WOMEN'S INSTITUTE

bread

LIZ HERBERT

SIMON &
SCHUSTER

LONDON · NEW YORK · SYDNEY · TORONTO

Acknowledgements

I would like to thank my family who, during the writing of this book, have put up with drastically disrupted routines. Their consolation – an abundance of samples on offer!

First published in Great Britain by Simon & Schuster UK Ltd, 2009
A CBS Company

Simon & Schuster UK Ltd
1st Floor, 222 Gray's Inn Road, London WC1X 8HB

The right of Liz Herbert to be identified as the Author of this Work has been asserted by her in accordance with sections 77 and 78 of the Copyright, Designs and Patents Act 1988.

1 3 5 7 9 10 8 6 4 2

Project editor: Nicki Lampon
Design: Tiger Media Ltd., Fiona Andreanelli
Food photography: Chris Alack
Styling: Jo Harris
Home economy: Lorna Brash

Printed and bound in China

ISBN 978-1-84737-399-1

Contents

Introduction

Bread forms a major part of our diet. It can be incorporated into every meal of the day – be it toast for breakfast, doughnuts with a cup of coffee, sandwiches at lunch time, a bun for tea or savoury bread to accompany a main meal.

Nowadays we are spoilt by the enormous variety of breads available. However, although mass-produced sliced bread is convenient, it is undoubtedly inferior to home-made. Making your own bread is both therapeutic and infectious! There is an undeniable satisfaction in the actual physical action of kneading the dough. This, coupled with the irresistible aroma of freshly baked bread, is reason enough to bake your own.

I hope that the following pages will inspire you to regularly incorporate bread making into your day, and to set aside a little time to create your own 'manna from heaven'.

Notes on the Recipes

All the recipes in this book have been made entirely by hand when testing. If using an electric mixer, food processor or bread machine, please refer to the manufacturer's instructions. If converting recipes for use in a bread machine, check the quantities carefully to make sure that your machine has enough capacity for the ingredients.

Always use exact measurements. Never mix imperial and metric quantities. If using metric measurements, add the final amount of liquid gradually to achieve a manageable dough.

The term 'scant' has been used in some recipes for the liquid. This means a little less than the quantity stated. You may not need the whole measure.

Fine sea salt is used throughout.

All breads are baked on the middle shelf of the oven unless stated otherwise.

Ingredients for Bread Making

It is very easy to detail all the dos and don'ts of how to create the perfect loaf. In the end it comes down to experience. However, it's also important to have some basic knowledge of the role of the main ingredients in bread making, and to appreciate how they interact and influence one another.

FLOUR

Wheat flour is best suited to bread making. Other flours contain a lower amount of gluten, and are often combined with wheat flour when making bread.

Wheat

Always choose flour specifically labelled for bread making as it has a high protein content. When water is added these proteins form gluten, and it is this that is responsible for forming the structure of the bread.

White bread flour is made from wheat that has had the bran and wheat germ removed during milling. Premium or very strong white bread flours are also available and produce a lighter, more aired bread. Wholemeal bread flour is much coarser, with a 'nutty' flavour. Stoneground wholemeal bread flour is just produced the old fashioned way, milled between two large, grooved stones. Brown bread flour is a combination of white and wholemeal flours and can be bought or mixed yourself at home. Breads made with wholemeal and brown flours need more water and produce a denser loaf. The dough requires less kneading but takes longer to prove.

Malted grain flours are based on a mixture of white and wholemeal flours with malted grains to give a nutty, slightly sweet loaf. Semolina is made from hard durum wheat (used for pasta) and can be added to a dough or used to dust baking sheets.

Spelt

Spelt is an ancient form of wheat and can be bought in wholemeal or white form. Dough made with spelt should only be kneaded for 4–5 minutes and tends to prove quickly.

Cornmeal

Known as cornmeal in the USA and polenta in Italy, the latter tends to be more coarsely ground. Cornmeal is not to be confused with cornflour. Milled from sweetcorn kernels, it is gluten free, making it popular for those unable to tolerate wheat or gluten.

Oats

For bread making oats are usually incorporated whole as rolled oats or used as oatmeal. Oats do contain some gluten.

Barley

Barley flour is sold mixed with wheat flour or can be bought on its own over the Internet. Try substituting one-quarter wheat flour for barley flour.

Rice

Rice flour does not contain any gluten. It is available in white or brown (wholegrain) form but makes bread rather dry, so use in conjunction with another variety of flour when making wheat free bread.

Rye

Rye is very popular in Eastern Europe and America and has a poor gluten content, resulting in a fairly dense, chewy loaf. It is valued in bread making for adding flavour and colour.

Gluten free

There are a variety of gluten free flours available, such as gram (chickpea), soya and potato, as well as blends of different flours that have been pre-mixed to give good all-round results. As with other flours, do make sure that the packet states that it is suitable for bread making.

YEAST

Yeast is the raising agent used to make bread. It is a living organism and thrives in a warm, moist, sugary atmosphere. Salt, fat and sugar all slow down its progress, and consequently a longer time needs to be allowed for proving. In order to try and minimise this, bread can sometimes be made using a starter batter. This gives the yeast a head start so that when the other ingredients are added it has already begun to work. It is important to measure yeast accurately. Too little results in a heavy, poorly risen loaf; too much and the dough collapses on baking.

There are three forms of yeast available:

Dried yeast needs to be reconstituted in liquid with a little sugar before it can be used. After 15–20 minutes in a warm place, the liquid should be bubbly and frothing.

Fast action dried yeast (also known as easy blend) is added directly to the flour. Its main advantage is that the dough only requires one rise, which cuts down on proving time. The granules are much smaller than dried yeast so, if substituting one for another, it is not possible to do a straight switch.

Fresh yeast is no longer widely available. Some bakers may be able to sell you a small amount. If so, wrap in paper and keep in an airtight container in the fridge for up to two weeks. It is usually stirred into the liquid and then added to the flour.

SUGAR

Sugar helps to start the yeast working. White sugar is usually added to white dough. Wholemeal and brown breads taste good if flavoured with a more natural sugar, such as honey or muscovado. Malt extract or molasses are also sometimes used. Larger quantities of sugar are added to sweet breads, making the dough stickier and creating the need for a longer proving. Sweetened breads tend to have a closer texture, more like cake.

SALT

Salt helps to regulate how fast the dough rises. The more salt, the longer the dough will take to prove. Too little salt and you will be left with a sticky, unmanageable dough.

FAT

Butter, oils (sunflower, vegetable, olive and speciality), lard or white vegetable fat can all be used in bread making. Fat helps to keep the bread fresh and has a softening effect. Large quantities inhibit the action of yeast, so proving times may have to be increased accordingly.

EGGS

Enriched breads have added egg, which gives a yellow colour and softens the bread. Eggs give an overall richness to the dough and help it stay fresher for longer.

LIQUID

Liquid must be added in order to hydrate the yeast and to bind all the ingredients together. Water is usually added to basic dough. Milk is often used for enriched doughs. Milk also helps to keep the bread fresher for longer and results in a softer crumb and crust. It is very important that any liquid is warm. If it is cold the yeast will not start working, and if it is too hot it will kill the yeast. The ideal temperature is 38°C (100°F).

BREAD MIXES

There are many bread mixes available. They contain flour, yeast, salt and flavourings, together with flour improvers and emulsifiers to ensure a good end result. Some will make basic breads, others include added flavourings. Most simply require the addition of water.

STARTER DOUGHS

True starter doughs, also known as sour doughs because of their flavour, are made from just flour and water left over a period of days. They draw on bacteria from the air to cultivate into a yeasty batter. Each day a little more flour and water are added to keep it active. Rye flour makes a particularly good starter as its natural sugars are more easily broken down than those in wheat.

The resulting dough is sometimes known as the 'mother' starter. About a quarter of this is added to a basic recipe. The dough is then made as usual but, at the end, a quarter is kept back, ready to form the basis of the next new batch. Hence some of the original sour dough lives on as part of the make up of many loaves to come.

Biga, used in Italian breads (see Italian Semolina Bread page 27), uses a modern-day method in which baker's yeast is used in both the starter batter and the dough to speed up the process while still achieving the sour dough taste – combining the best of both worlds.

Stages of Bread Making

MIXING

A large bowl is usually best, but some people prefer to mix the dough on the work surface itself. In both cases, the liquid ingredients are poured into the dry ones, which are gradually incorporated. A wooden fork is ideal for mixing but use your hands to bring the last bits of flour together, leaving the sides of the bowl clean.

KNEADING

Bread dough is kneaded to develop the gluten in the flour, making it strong and elastic. White breads take longer to knead (about 10 minutes) than wholemeal and brown (about 5 minutes). The dough should end up silky and smooth.

To knead, place the dough on a work surface. Place both hands under the side furthest away and bring the dough towards you, folding it over to meet the near edge. Push down hard to seal, give it a quarter turn and repeat the action. You will gradually become faster and build up a rocking rhythm. Use the heel of your hand to push down. However, if you are working with relatively wet, sticky dough, it is easier to 'massage' it with your fingers, using both hands. It is not necessary to flour the work surface; in time the dough will become less sticky. However, if the dough is still sticky after 10 minutes, wash and dry your hands, lightly flour them and knead the dough just until it forms a ball.

PROVING

Dough needs to be proved (left to rise) in order to give the yeast an opportunity to work. A warm environment of about 32°C (90°F) is ideal – try an airing cupboard, a spot close to the boiler or a top oven with the one below switched on.

The dough should be left until it is about double its original size. This usually takes 1–1½ hours for white dough, longer for wholemeal and enriched breads. It is not possible to be specific as temperatures will fluctuate. If it is too cold the dough will take a long time to prove. If it is too hot the yeast will be killed and you will end up with a heavy, flat loaf. Dough left to rise slowly will have a better flavour, whereas those proved too quickly tend not to keep for so long and have a crumbly texture.

It is important to cover the dough so it does not dry out. A large, oiled polythene bag is good, or place the dough in a lightly oiled, clean bowl and cover with a clean, damp tea towel or cling film.

A recipe will have one or two provings. Fast action dried yeasts cut out the need to prove the dough twice. However, doing so will result in a denser loaf that has less flavour. The second proving will take about 45 minutes for loaves and 30 minutes for rolls. It should be slightly sticky to the touch when ready.

Knowledge of how temperature affects yeast gives you more control over your bread making, enabling you to slow down or speed up proving times to fit in with your schedule. If you halve the amount of yeast you use, you can even leave dough in the fridge for up to 12 hours. Bring it back to room temperature before shaping.

KNOCKING BACK

This is the term used for giving the dough a second, shorter kneading after it has proved. The purpose is to knock out air, which would lead to an uneven loaf with large air holes. The dough should be kneaded for a few minutes until it feels firm. After knocking back, the dough is shaped and put in a tin or on a baking sheet.

FINISHING TOUCHES

It is important to handle the dough very gently at the final stage to avoid knocking out any air and creating a dense, heavy bread.

Shaping
Some breads have a traditional finish, the shape being as much a part of the final bread as the ingredients. A good way to experiment is to divide a batch of basic dough into pieces and to shape them in different ways.

Cutting
Cuts can be made 1 cm (½ inch) deep with a very sharp knife before or after the dough has been proved and shaped.

Glazing
Certain glazes are associated with savoury bread and others with sweet breads. Likewise for wholemeal and white-based doughs. They may be applied before or after baking.

Topping
Toppings improve the appearance of the bread and add flavour and texture. They vary from a dusting of flour to a sprinkling of cereal flakes or grains, seeds, chopped nuts, herbs, coarse sea salt and grated cheese. Sweet breads are often topped with some form of sugar.

Crusts
Sugar and salt glazes both make the crust thicker.

A hard crust can be created by either spraying inside the oven with a fine mister a couple of minutes before you put in the dough or by placing a tin of boiling water on the bottom shelf when you turn the oven on. Be very careful when you open the oven as the steam will rush out. Alternatively, brush the crust with salted water or open the oven door for the last 5 minutes of baking.

A soft crust can be created by dusting the loaf with flour before baking, wrapping the bread in a clean, dry tea towel as soon as you take it out of the oven or adding fat and sugar to the dough. If you like a crisp crust, remove the bread from the oven 5 minutes before the end of its cooking time, take it out of the tin and return it to the oven on a baking tray.

BAKING

Always preheat the oven – too low a temperature and the dough will continue to prove, spilling over the tin. To test whether the bread is done, tap the bottom – it should sound hollow. Enriched breads are susceptible to burning and may need to be covered with foil or greaseproof paper after about 10 minutes.

STORING

Home made bread is best eaten warm or on the same day as baking. As soon as the bread is cooled, wrap in a paper bag or linen bread bag and store in a bread bin in a cool, dry place. Alternatively, seal in a polythene bag to keep fresh. Don't keep bread in the fridge.

It is always a good idea to double the quantity and put one loaf in the freezer. Wrap in a polythene bag and freeze as soon as it has cooled. Bread will keep for about 3 months, although crusty bread does not freeze well as the crust tends to flake off. To refresh day-old or defrosted bread, heat in a preheated oven at Gas Mark 4/180°C/350°F for 8–10 minutes.

BREAD MACHINES

There is no standard formula for converting recipes for use in a bread machine. Start with the recipes in the manufacturer's booklet. Once you become confident, these recipes can be adapted for use. The main thing is to check that the capacity of your bread maker matches the quantity of ingredients in the recipe. Remember that only fast action dried yeast is suitable for use in bread machines. Dough can also be mixed, kneaded and left to rise in a bread machine, then turned out on to a work surface to be shaped by hand, giving a home-made finish.

RESCUE REMEDIES

Poor rise and a heavy, close texture
The yeast was stale.
Too little yeast was used or it was not given enough time to work.
The liquid was too hot.
Too much salt was added.
The dough was not kneaded for long enough.

'Stretch marks' around the sides
The dough was under proved.

Dough spills over the tin
Too much dough was used for the size of the tin (generally bread made using 450 g/1 lb flour will need to be baked in a 900 g/2 lb tin).
Too much yeast was used.

Flat top
Not enough salt was used.
Too soft a flour was used.
The dough was over proved.
The dough was not properly shaped.

Sunken loaf
The loaf was undercooked.
Too much liquid was used.
Not enough salt was used.
The dough was over proved.

Large holes and uneven textured bread
The dough was not knocked back properly.

Sour, yeasty smell
The dough was over proved.
The yeast was old and 'going off'.
Too much yeast was used.

Crumbly crumb
The dough was put in too warm a place to rise.
Too soft a flour was used.
Too much yeast was used.
The dough was over proved.

Basic Breads

If you have never made bread before, or are in need of a refresher course, then this chapter is a good starting point. People are often wary of making bread, but the more bread you make, the better you become at judging whether the dough is right or not. Once the basics have been mastered, variations are often little more than fancy shaping. As with most things, with a little know-how you will find that complicated-looking breads are actually fairly simple. With practice comes experience, and with experience comes confidence.

French Country Bread, page 22

Basic White Bread (Farmhouse Loaf)

Makes: *1 loaf* **Preparation time:** *20 minutes + proving + 30–35 minutes baking*
Freezing: *recommended*

Try developing your own breads, using this recipe as a base and adding ingredients to create a sweet or savoury loaf.

---

450 g (1 lb) strong white bread flour, plus extra for dusting
25 g (1 oz) butter
1 teaspoon sugar
1 teaspoon salt
1 teaspoon fast action dried yeast
300 ml (½ pint) hand-hot water

1 Put the flour in a large mixing bowl and rub in the butter. Stir in the sugar, salt and yeast. Make a well in the centre, pour the water in all at once and mix well to combine the ingredients. After a little while it is easiest to dispense with the stirring utensil and use your hands to bring the dough together.

2 Turn out on to an unfloured surface and knead (page 8) the dough. It will take about 10 minutes for it to lose its 'craggy' appearance and take on a silky smoothness.

3 Place the dough in a large polythene bag that has been lightly oiled. Seal, allowing plenty of room for the dough to expand, and prove (page 8) in a warm place for about an hour or until it has doubled in size.

4 Grease a 900 g (2 lb) loaf tin and dust with flour.

5 Knock back (page 9) the dough for 2–3 minutes, making sure that all the air is dispelled. Shape into an oblong by putting both hands under the piece of dough furthest away and bringing it towards you, folding it over the rest of the dough. Push down to seal the edge nearest you. Give the dough a quarter turn and repeat until you have a smooth-shaped oblong. Lay it in the prepared tin, seam side down. Cover and leave to prove until doubled in size (about 45 minutes).

6 Preheat the oven to Gas Mark 8/230°C/450°F.

7 Using a very sharp knife, make a 1 cm (½ inch) deep cut down the centre of the loaf. Dust liberally with flour.

8 Bake for 30–35 minutes. If your baking tin is high and short, place the loaf one shelf below the centre of the oven. Longer, shallower loaf tins should be baked on the middle shelf.

9 Remove the bread from the tin and transfer to a wire rack to cool. The loaf should sound hollow on the bottom when tapped.

Tips: Do not flour the work surface. The dough becomes less sticky as you work it and the flour absorbs moisture. Adding too much flour at this stage results in a dry dough.

If you like a crisp crust, remove the loaf from the tin when baked, place it on a baking tray and return it to the oven for a further 5 minutes.

Easy Brown Bread

Makes: *1 loaf* **Preparation time:** *15 minutes + proving + 30–35 minutes baking*
Freezing: *recommended*

Brown bread is probably the best bread to make as an introduction to bread making as the dough handles beautifully. It does not require as long a kneading time as white bread and this recipe only rises once, so the dough is just mixed, kneaded, shaped, proved and baked.

300 g (10 oz) **strong white bread flour**
300 g (10 oz) **strong wholemeal bread flour**
25 g (1 oz) **white vegetable fat**
  or sunflower oil
1¼ teaspoons **sugar**
1¼ teaspoons **salt**
1¼ teaspoons **fast action dried yeast**
375 ml (13 fl oz) **hand-hot water**

1 Grease a 900 g (2 lb) loaf tin.

2 Combine the flours in a large mixing bowl. Rub in the fat and stir in the sugar, salt and yeast. Make a well in the centre (if using oil, add at this stage) and pour in the water. Gradually incorporate the dry ingredients, mixing to a soft dough. Use your hands to bring the last crumbs together.

3 Turn out on to an unfloured surface and knead (page 8) for about 5 minutes until smooth.

4 Shape the dough into an oblong by putting both hands under the piece of dough furthest away and bringing it towards you, folding it over the rest of the dough. Push down to seal the edge nearest you. Give the dough a quarter turn and repeat until you have a smooth-shaped oblong. Lay it in the prepared tin, seam side down. Using a sharp knife, make a cut down the centre of the loaf. Place the tin in an oiled polythene bag and prove (page 8) in a warm place until doubled in size.

5 Preheat the oven to Gas Mark 8/230°C/450°F.

6 Bake for 30–35 minutes. If your baking tin is high and short, place the loaf one shelf below the centre of the oven. Longer, shallower loaf tins should be baked on the middle shelf.

7 Turn out on to a wire rack. The bottom should sound hollow when tapped. For a crisp crust, leave out of the tin and return to the oven for a further 5 minutes.

Note: Slightly more flour is used than in the basic white bread recipe, as brown and wholemeal varieties do not rise to the same extent as white loaves.

Wheatgerm Bread

Makes: *1 loaf* **Preparation time:** *15 minutes + proving + 30–35 minutes baking*
Freezing: *recommended*

Wheatgerm gives this bread a wonderful golden crumb, as well as boosting its nutritional value.

225 g (8 oz) strong wholemeal bread flour
225 g (8 oz) strong white bread flour
50 g (2 oz) wheatgerm
1 tablespoon muscovado sugar
1 teaspoon salt
1 teaspoon fast action dried yeast
2 tablespoons sunflower oil
325–350 ml (11–12 fl oz) hand-hot water

1 Lightly grease a 900 g (2 lb) loaf tin.

2 Combine the flours, wheatgerm, sugar, salt and yeast in a large mixing bowl. Make a well in the centre and add the oil and water. Mix to a soft dough.

3 Turn the dough out on to an unfloured surface and knead (page 8) for about 5 minutes until smooth.

4 Shape the dough into an oblong by putting both hands under the piece of dough furthest away and bringing it towards you, folding it over the rest of the dough. Push down to seal the edge nearest you. Give the dough a quarter turn and repeat until you have a smooth-shaped oblong. Lay it in the prepared tin, seam side down. Using a sharp knife, make a cut down the centre of the loaf. Cover and prove (page 8) in a warm place until doubled in size.

5 Preheat the oven to Gas Mark 7/220°C/425°F.

6 Bake the bread one shelf below the middle of the oven for 30–35 minutes. Remove from the tin and cool on a wire rack.

White Seeded Loaf

Makes: *1 loaf* **Preparation time:** *25 minutes + proving + 25–30 minutes baking*
Freezing: *recommended*

In this loaf, six types of seed are mixed into the dough to create a
bread full of flavour and crunch.

450 g (1 lb) strong white bread flour
1 teaspoon sugar
1 teaspoon salt
1 teaspoon fast action dried yeast
1 tablespoon each of sesame, linseed, millet,
    pumpkin, poppy and sunflower seeds
1 tablespoon sunflower oil
scant 300 ml (½ pint) hand-hot water (page 4)
For the topping:
milk
2 teaspoons mixed seeds

1 Combine the flour, sugar, salt, yeast and
seeds in a bowl. Make a well in the centre and
add the oil and water. Mix to a soft dough.

2 Turn the dough out on to an unfloured surface
and knead (page 8) for about 10 minutes until
smooth. Place in an oiled polythene bag and
prove (page 8) in a warm place until doubled
in size.

3 Grease a baking sheet.

4 Knock back (page 9) the dough for a few
minutes to knock out all the air. Shape into a
round. Place on the baking sheet and, using
a sharp knife, slash three lines across the top
to a depth of about 1 cm (½ inch). Cover and
prove until doubled in size.

5 Preheat the oven to Gas Mark 7/220°C/425°F.

6 Brush the surface of the dough with milk and
sprinkle with seeds. Bake for 25–30 minutes
until golden. Cool on a wire rack.

Tip: If you prefer, use just one variety of seed,
or a mixture of two or three favourites.

Wholemeal Stoneground Loaf

Makes: *1 loaf* **Preparation time:** *15 minutes + proving + 30–35 minutes baking*
Freezing: *recommended*

Adding a little more yeast than normal helps to lighten wholemeal and stoneground loaves. Alternatively, substitute some of the wholemeal flour with white bread flour.

**550 g (1¼ lbs) strong wholemeal or
  stoneground bread flour
1 teaspoon brown sugar
1 teaspoon salt
1¼ teaspoons fast action dried yeast
2 tablespoons sunflower or vegetable oil
375–400 ml (13–14 fl oz) hand-hot water**

1 Combine the flour, sugar, salt and yeast in a large mixing bowl. Make a well in the centre and add the oil and enough water to bind the ingredients together. Using a wooden spoon, mix to a soft dough, gradually drawing in the dry ingredients. When it is almost mixed, put aside the spoon and use your hands to form a ball of dough.

2 Turn out on to an unfloured work surface and knead (page 8) for about 5 minutes until smooth. Place in a lightly oiled polythene bag and leave in a warm place to prove (page 8) until the dough has doubled in size. This can take 1–1½ hours.

3 Grease a 900 g (2 lb) loaf tin.

4 Turn the dough out again and knead for a few minutes to knock out the air. Shape into an oblong with the short end nearest to you. Putting your fingertips under the piece of dough furthest away, bring the dough towards you, folding it in half. Press down, then give the dough a quarter turn. Repeat this, shaping several times until you have a smooth-shaped oblong. Place in the prepared tin, seam side down.

5 Cover and leave in a warm place to prove until the bread rises to just above the top of the tin.

6 Preheat the oven to Gas Mark 7/220°C/425°F.

7 Bake for 30–35 minutes one shelf below the middle of the oven if you have a short, squat tin, or on the centre shelf if you have a longer, shallow tin.

8 Remove from the tin and cool on a wire rack. The loaf should sound hollow on the bottom when tapped. If you prefer a crisp crust, then place the bread on a baking tray and return to the oven for a further 5 minutes.

Tip: If you would like to make a good sized cob loaf, simply shape the knocked back dough into a round, mark with a cross and, after a second proving, bake in the centre of the oven for 25–30 minutes.

Malted Mixed Grain Bread

Makes: *1 loaf* **Preparation time:** *15 minutes + proving + 25 minutes baking*
Freezing: *recommended*

This is a fairly dense, slightly sweet, chewy bread packed with flavour.

450 g (1 lb) malted grain bread flour
1 teaspoon salt
1 teaspoon fast action dried yeast
2 tablespoons malt extract
2 tablespoons sunflower oil
275 ml (9 fl oz) hand-hot water

1 Lightly grease a baking sheet.

2 Combine the flour, salt and yeast in a bowl. Make a well in the centre and add the malt extract, oil and water. Mix to a soft dough.

3 Turn out on to an unfloured surface and knead (page 8) for about 10 minutes until smooth. The malt makes this dough very sticky – do not panic! Keep working it the best you can and you will be left with a beautifully soft dough.

4 Give the work surface a good scrape down. Scrub any dough off your hands and then dust them with a little flour. Form the dough into a sausage shape about 20 cm (8 inches) in length. Place the dough on the baking sheet, cover and prove (page 8) in a warm place until doubled in size.

5 Preheat the oven to Gas Mark 8/230°C/450°F.

6 Bake for 25 minutes until the loaf sounds hollow when tapped on the base. Cool on a wire rack.

Milk Bread (Bridge Rolls)

Makes: *18 rolls* **Preparation time:** *25 minutes + proving + 15 minutes baking*
Freezing: *recommended*

Soft and golden, these little rolls are perfect for filling with sausages, caramelised onions and relish. Space them on the baking sheet so that they are almost touching and you will end up with soft-sided, tall rolls.

450 g (1 lb) strong white bread flour
50 g (2 oz) butter
1 tablespoon caster sugar
1 teaspoon salt
1 teaspoon fast action dried yeast
300 ml (½ pint) warm semi-skimmed milk

1 Put the flour in a large mixing bowl and rub in the butter. Stir in the sugar, salt and yeast and mix to a soft dough with the milk.

2 Turn out on to an unfloured surface and knead (page 8) for about 10 minutes until smooth. Cover and prove (page 8) in a warm place until doubled in size.

3 Grease a baking sheet.

4 Divide the dough into 18 pieces, each weighing approximately 40 g (1½ oz). Keep them covered while you shape one at a time.

5 Using your fingertips, roll each piece of dough out into an 8 cm (3¼ inch) long sausage shape. Arrange the rolls in two rows on the baking sheet, side by side and almost touching. Cover and prove.

6 Preheat the oven to Gas Mark 6/200°C/400°F.

7 Bake the rolls for 15 minutes. Remove from the oven to a wire rack and cover with a clean tea towel so that they have a traditional soft crust.

Tip: The same quantity of dough can also be used in mini individual tins to produce soft rolls that are perfect for a dinner party.

French Country Bread

Makes: *1 loaf* **Preparation time:** *20 minutes + 1–2 days fermenting + proving + 30–35 minutes baking* **Freezing:** *recommended*

This classic, rustic style French loaf, made with white and wholemeal flours, has a sour taste achieved by fermenting the yeast a day or two before making the bread.

175 g (6 oz) strong white bread flour, plus
    extra for dusting
175 g (6 oz) strong wholemeal bread flour
25 g (1 oz) butter
1 teaspoon salt
½ teaspoon fast action dried yeast
175 ml (6 fl oz) hand-hot water
For the starter dough:
115 g (4 oz) strong white bread flour
½ teaspoon fast action dried yeast
150 ml (¼ pint) warm water

1 Begin the starter dough 24–48 hours before making the bread. Combine the flour for the starter dough with the yeast and stir in the water to make a thick batter. Cover with a damp tea towel and leave in a cool place to ferment for 1–2 days. Stir occasionally, and check frequently to make sure that the tea towel remains damp.

2 When you are ready to make the actual bread, combine the flours in a bowl. Rub in the butter. Stir in the salt, yeast, starter dough and water and mix to form a soft dough.

3 Turn out on to an unfloured surface and knead (page 8) for 8–10 minutes until smooth. Cover and prove (page 8) in a warm place until doubled in size.

4 Grease a baking sheet and dust with flour.

5 Knock back (page 9) the dough and form into a round. Place on the baking sheet and, using a sharp knife, slash the surface with 4–5 deep lines one way and then the other. This will give you a diamond effect. Cover and prove.

6 Preheat the oven to Gas Mark 6/200°C/400°F.

7 Dust the loaf liberally with flour and bake for 30–35 minutes until golden and crisp. Cool on a wire rack.

Illustrated on page 13

Rye Bread

Makes: *1 loaf* **Preparation time:** *20 minutes + proving + 25–30 minutes baking*
Freezing: *recommended*

Rye flour has a low gluten content and produces a loaf with quite a close, dense texture. It has a distinctive 'chewiness' to it.

225 g (8 oz) wholemeal rye flour, plus extra for dusting
225 g (8 oz) strong white bread flour
1½ teaspoons salt
1½ teaspoons fast action dried yeast
1½ teaspoons caraway seeds
2 tablespoons molasses sugar
325–350 ml (11–12 fl oz) hand-hot water

1 Combine the flours in a large mixing bowl. Stir in the salt, yeast and caraway seeds. Rub the molasses sugar through the mixture to remove any lumps. Add the water and mix to a soft dough.

2 Turn out on to an unfloured surface and knead (page 8) for approximately 8 minutes until smooth. Cover and prove (page 8) in a warm place until doubled in size.

3 Grease a baking sheet.

4 Knock back (page 9) the dough for a couple of minutes to distribute any air bubbles, then shape into a log or round. Place on the baking sheet and slash a single deep line down the length of the dough, slightly off centre. Dust with a little flour if wished. Cover and prove.

5 Preheat the oven to Gas Mark 7/220°C/425°F.

6 Bake the bread for 25–30 minutes. Cool on a wire rack.

Tip: Rye bread usually contains caraway seeds. This recipe contains just enough to give the bread a little flavour; you may wish to increase the quantity if you prefer a stronger taste.

Barley Bread

Makes: *1 loaf* **Preparation time:** *45 minutes + 20 minutes cooking + proving + 30–35 minutes baking* **Freezing:** *recommended*

Barley is an old style grain that now only tends to be used in casseroles and malt extract. This bread uses barley in its flour and grain form, resulting in a moist, textured loaf, full of flavour. I have used a flour mix, Barleycorn. If you wish to make your own mix, you can buy pure barley flour on the Internet.

50 g (2 oz) pearl barley
350 g (12 oz) Barleycorn bread flour
¾ teaspoon salt
¾ teaspoon fast action dried yeast
2 teaspoons runny honey
1 tablespoon sunflower oil
175 ml (6 fl oz) hand-hot water

1 Rinse the pearl barley. Place it in a small saucepan and cover with plenty of cold water. Bring to the boil and simmer for 20 minutes. Drain and run under cold water to cool. Turn out on to a plate lined with several sheets of kitchen paper to drain thoroughly.

2 Combine the Barleycorn flour, salt and yeast in a bowl. Make a well in the centre and add the honey, oil, water and cooked barley. Mix to a soft dough.

3 Turn out on to an unfloured surface and knead (page 8) for 8–10 minutes until smooth. Cover and leave to rise slowly at room temperature until doubled in size. The slower rise helps develop the flavour.

4 Grease a 900 g (2 lb) loaf tin.

5 Knock back (page 9) the dough and shape into an oblong by putting both hands under the piece of dough furthest away and bringing it towards you, folding it over the rest of the dough. Push down to seal the edge nearest you. Give the dough a quarter turn and repeat until you have a smooth-shaped oblong. Place in the tin, cover and leave to rise slowly for about 1 hour.

6 Preheat the oven to Gas Mark 7/220°C/425°F.

7 Bake for 30–35 minutes on one rung below the centre of the oven. Cool on a wire rack.

Tip: This can also be shaped in a more rustic way by lining a basket or tin with a clean linen tea towel, dusting it with flour, placing the shaped dough inside, sprinkling a little more flour on top and folding the tea towel over to encase it. Once the dough has doubled in size carefully tip out on to a greased baking sheet and cook as above but on the middle shelf of the oven.

Wholemeal Spelt Bread

Makes: *1 loaf* **Preparation time:** *20 minutes + proving + 35–40 minutes baking*
Freezing: *recommended*

Spelt flour used to be very popular, but went into decline when manufacturing costs increased due to the difficulty in separating the tough husk from the grain. Now enjoying a revival, both white and wholemeal varieties are available. Although a cousin to wheat flour, its protein structure is different, and consequently some people who have an intolerance to wheat may be able to eat spelt.

450 g (1 lb) stoneground strong spelt bread
   flour, plus extra for dusting
25 g (1 oz) butter
1 teaspoon muscovado sugar
1 teaspoon salt
1½ teaspoons fast action dried yeast
300–325 ml (10–11 fl oz) hand-hot water

1 Lightly grease a 900 g (2 lb) loaf tin.

2 Put the flour in a large mixing bowl and rub in the butter. Stir in the sugar, salt and yeast and mix to a soft dough with the water.

3 Turn out on to an unfloured surface and knead (page 8) for 4 minutes only. Shape into an oblong by putting both hands under the piece of dough furthest away and bringing it towards you, folding it over the rest of the dough. Push down to seal the edge nearest you. Give the dough a quarter turn and repeat until you have a smooth-shaped oblong. Place in the prepared loaf tin. Cover and prove (page 8) in a warm place until doubled in size.

4 Preheat the oven to Gas Mark 7/220°C/425°F.

5 Dust the bread with flour and bake for 35–40 minutes. Turn out on to a wire rack to cool.

Tip: Spelt has a more delicate gluten structure than wheat flour, so the dough does not require such a long kneading time. It also tends to rise more quickly than ordinary bread, so keep an eye on it and bake as soon as the loaf has doubled in size.

Italian Semolina Bread

Makes: *1 loaf* **Preparation time:** *25 minutes + 24–36 hours standing + proving + 35–40 minutes baking* **Freezing:** *recommended*

This is an Italian form of sour dough bread made with a 'biga' starter. There is nothing rushed about this bread – it also has a long first proving to allow the alcohols given off by the yeast to flavour the dough.

225 g (8 oz) fine semolina, plus extra for
    sprinkling
225 g (8 oz) strong white bread flour, plus
    extra for dusting
115 g (4 oz) strong wholemeal bread flour
1½ teaspoons salt
1 teaspoon fast action dried yeast
2 tablespoons olive oil
350 ml (12 fl oz) hand-hot water
For the biga:
115 g (4 oz) strong white bread flour
½ teaspoon fast action dried yeast
150 ml (¼ pint) hand-hot water

1 Prepare the biga the day before you wish to make the bread. Place the flour and yeast in a small bowl and blend in the water to make a paste. Cover with a damp tea towel and leave in a cool place for 24–36 hours.

2 The next day, place the semolina and flours in a large bowl and stir in the salt and yeast. Make a well in the centre, add 115 g (4 oz) of the biga, the olive oil and the water. Mix to a soft dough.

3 Turn out on to an unfloured surface and knead (page 8) for 8–10 minutes until smooth. Cover and prove (page 8) at room temperature until doubled in size – this takes about 2 hours.

4 Knock back (page 9) the dough and shape into a round.

5 Dust a linen tea towel with flour and use it to line a large mixing bowl. Place the dough inside, with the smooth side facing down. Dust with a little flour and fold over the tea towel to encase the dough. Prove slowly at room temperature until doubled in size.

6 Preheat the oven to Gas Mark 7/220°C/425°F. Grease a baking sheet and sprinkle with a little semolina.

7 Very carefully tip the dough out on to the baking sheet. Using a sharp knife, slash lines across the top to make a diamond effect. Dust with a little white flour.

8 Bake for 35–40 minutes, opening the oven door for the final 5 minutes if you like a crisp crust. Cool on a wire rack.

Rice Bread

Makes: *1 loaf* **Preparation time:** *25 minutes + proving + 15 minutes cooking + 30 minutes baking*
Freezing: *recommended*

The beauty of breads with added cooked grain (such as Barley Bread, page 24) is that, unlike most home-made breads that are stale in a day or two, the grain helps keep the loaf moist. This milk bread is a particular favourite with children, and is lovely spread with butter and jam.

40 g (1½ oz) Arborio or risotto rice
¾ teaspoon salt, plus extra for rice
350 g (12 oz) strong white bread flour
1 teaspoon fast action dried yeast
$^1/_8$ teaspoon freshly grated nutmeg
1 tablespoon runny honey
25 g (1 oz) butter, softened
1 teaspoon vanilla essence
225 ml (8 fl oz) warm semi-skimmed milk, plus
   extra to glaze

1 Place the rice in a small pan. Cover with water, add a little salt, bring to the boil and simmer for 15 minutes. Drain and run under a cold tap to cool. Transfer to a double thickness of kitchen paper to remove any excess water.

2 Combine the flour, salt, yeast and nutmeg in a bowl. Stir in the cooked rice. Make a well in the centre and add the honey, butter, vanilla essence and milk. Mix to a soft dough.

3 Turn out on to an unfloured surface and knead (page 8) for 8–10 minutes until smooth. Place in an oiled polythene bag and prove (page 8) in a warm place until doubled in size.

4 Grease a 900 g (2 lb) loaf tin.

5 Knock back (page 9) the dough and form into an oblong by putting both hands under the piece of dough furthest away and bringing it towards you, folding it over the rest of the dough. Push down to seal the edge nearest you. Give the dough a quarter turn and repeat until you have a smooth-shaped oblong. Place in the prepared tin, cover and prove until doubled in size.

6 Preheat the oven to Gas Mark 7/220°C/425°F.

7 Brush the loaf with a little milk and bake for about 30 minutes. Leave in the tin for 5 minutes before turning out on to a wire rack to cool.

Honey and Oat Bread

Makes: *1 loaf* **Preparation time:** *15 minutes + proving + 30 minutes baking*
Freezing: *recommended*

Honey gives this bread a lovely golden, thick crust, full of flavour, and a delicious lightly sweetened taste. Sweet and savoury toppings go well with this loaf. Once it is a day old it is best eaten toasted.

350 g (12 oz) strong white bread flour
80 g (3 oz) medium oatmeal, plus extra for
   sprinkling
50 g (2 oz) rolled oats, plus extra for sprinkling
1 teaspoon salt
1½ teaspoons fast action dried yeast
3 tablespoons runny honey
2 tablespoons sunflower oil
225–250 ml (8–9 fl oz) warm semi-skimmed
   milk, plus extra to glaze

1 Grease a 900 g (2 lb) oblong loaf tin and sprinkle lightly with a little oatmeal and rolled oats.

2 Combine the flour, oatmeal, oats, salt and yeast in a large bowl. Make a well in the centre and add the honey, oil and warm milk. Mix to a soft dough.

3 Turn out on to an unfloured surface and knead (page 8) for 8–10 minutes until smooth.

4 Shape into an oblong by putting both hands under the piece of dough furthest away and bringing it towards you, folding it over the rest of the dough. Push down to seal the edge nearest you. Give the dough a quarter turn and repeat until you have a smooth-shaped oblong. Place in the prepared tin, brush with a little milk and sprinkle with oatmeal and rolled oats. Cover and prove (page 8) in a warm place until doubled in size.

5 Preheat the oven to Gas Mark 7/220°C/425°F.

6 Bake the bread for about 30 minutes until golden. Remove from the tin and cool on a wire rack.

Polenta Bread

Makes: *1 loaf* **Preparation time:** *15 minutes + proving + 25 minutes*
Freezing: *recommended*

Polenta (or maize flour) has a slightly grainy texture and a vivid yellow colour that makes an everyday loaf a little more interesting.

350 g (12 oz) strong white bread flour
115 g (4 oz) polenta, plus extra for sprinkling
1 teaspoon sugar
1 teaspoon salt
1 teaspoon fast action dried yeast
25 g (1 oz) butter, melted
275–300 ml (9–10 fl oz) hand-hot water

1 Combine the flour, polenta, sugar, salt and yeast in a mixing bowl. Add the butter and water and mix to a soft dough.

2 Turn out on to an unfloured surface and knead (page 8) for 8–10 minutes until smooth. Cover and prove (page 8) in a warm place until doubled in size.

3 Grease a baking sheet and sprinkle with polenta.

4 Knock back (page 9) the dough and shape into an 18 cm (7 inch) long oval. Place on the baking sheet. Using a sharp knife, make deep cuts on alternate sides of the loaf, roughly equidistant, starting two thirds across the top, and finishing on the baking tray.

5 Cover and prove until doubled in size.

6 Preheat the oven to Gas Mark 7/220°C/425°F.

7 Sprinkle liberally with polenta and bake for about 25 minutes until golden. Cool on a wire rack.

Soya Flour Bread

Makes: *1 loaf* **Preparation time:** *20 minutes + proving + 30 minutes baking*
Freezing: *recommended*

Soya flour is not an obvious choice for making bread, but it does create a lovely golden loaf with a soft, cake-like crumb that keeps well for a couple of days. Soya flour is readily available from health food shops.

300 g (10 oz) strong white bread flour
80 g (3 oz) soya flour
80 g (3 oz) wholemeal rye flour
1 teaspoon muscovado sugar
1 teaspoon salt
1¼ teaspoons fast action dried yeast
2 tablespoons sunflower oil
300–325 ml (10–11 fl oz) hand-hot water
For the topping:
1 egg
1 tablespoon water
a handful of golden linseeds

1 Combine the flours in a large mixing bowl with the sugar, salt and yeast. Make a well in the centre and stir in the oil and water to make a soft dough.

2 Turn out on to a floured surface and knead (page 8) for 8–10 minutes until smooth. Cover and prove (page 8) in a warm place until doubled in size.

3 Grease a 900 g (2 lb) loaf tin.

4 Knock back (page 9) the dough and shape into an oblong by putting both hands under the piece of dough furthest away and bringing it towards you, folding it over the rest of the dough. Push down to seal the edge nearest you. Give the dough a quarter turn and repeat until you have a smooth-shaped oblong. Place in the prepared tin, cover and prove until doubled in size.

5 Preheat the oven to Gas Mark 7/220°C/425°F.

6 Beat the egg with the water and brush the loaf with the egg glaze. Sprinkle linseeds liberally over the surface. Bake one shelf below the middle of the oven for 30 minutes. Cool on a wire rack.

Tip: Soya makes this bread quite sticky to work with, so you may need to sprinkle a little flour periodically on to the work surface whilst kneading.

Plain and Savoury

One of the great advantages of bread making is how a few standard ingredients can be built upon to make so many different variations. This chapter begins with basic breads that use very few ingredients other than the essentials. Shaping the dough in different ways means you can produce a wide range of alternative breads. Then, by adding other ingredients, the scope widens still further to produce a wealth of delicious alternatives.

Sweet Chestnut Bread, page 59

French Bread

Makes: *2 baguettes* **Preparation time:** *20 minutes + proving + 20 minutes baking*
Freezing: *recommended*

Some plain flour is mixed in with bread flour in this recipe to provide a texture more reminiscent of true French bread, which is traditionally made with French flour.

350 g (12 oz) strong white bread flour, plus extra for dusting
115 g (4 oz) plain white flour
1 teaspoon sugar
1 teaspoon salt
1½ teaspoons fast action dried yeast
300 ml (½ pint) hand-hot water

1 Combine the flours, sugar, salt and yeast in a large bowl. Add the water and mix to a soft dough.

2 Turn out on to an unfloured work surface and knead (page 8) for about 10 minutes until smooth. Cover and prove (page 8) in a warm place until doubled in size.

3 Grease and flour two baking sheets.

4 Divide the dough into two equal pieces. Without knocking back, roll out on a lightly floured surface to a rectangle measuring 38 x 30 cm (15 x 12 inches). Roll up tightly from the long edge, pinching the seams together. Place diagonally on the baking sheets, seam side down, and make deep, diagonal cuts at 6 cm (2½ inch) intervals. Prove, uncovered, until doubled in size.

5 Preheat the oven to Gas Mark 7/220°C/425°F. Place a large, shallow dish on the bottom shelf of the oven and carefully half fill this with boiling water.

6 Dust the baguettes with a little flour and bake for 20 minutes, until golden. Cool on a wire rack and eat the same day.

Tips: The water in the oven will create steam, which will give the bread a crisp crust. Be very careful to stand well back when you open the oven, otherwise the steam may catch you in the face.

This recipe produces a loaf with a matt finish. If you prefer your bread to be shiny, brush the dough with an egg white, beaten with 1 tablespoon water.

Pitta Bread

Makes: *6 breads* **Preparation time:** *25 minutes + proving + 6–8 minutes baking*
Freezing: *recommended*

Pitta bread is a very basic bread, made from just a few simple
ingredients. I have recommended quite a short cooking time.
This does not brown the breads as they are often toasted
before eating.

350 g (12 oz) strong white bread flour, plus
   extra for dusting
½ teaspoon sugar
¾ teaspoon salt
¾ teaspoon fast action dried yeast
225 ml (8 fl oz) hand-hot water

Tip: These are delicious filled with hot or
cold meats and salad, or sliced into strips to
accompany dips.

1 Combine the flour, sugar, salt and yeast in a
  bowl. Stir in the water to make a soft dough.

2 Turn out on to an unfloured work surface and
  knead (page 8) for 10 minutes until smooth.
  Rest the dough for 10 minutes.

3 Dust two baking sheets with flour.

4 Divide the dough into six equal pieces. On a
  lightly floured surface, roll out each piece into
  a 20 cm (8 inch) by 12 cm (4½ inches) oval.
  Score a line across the centre of each to make
  the breads easier to tear. Place well apart on
  the baking sheets, cover and prove (page 8)
  for 20 minutes only, until they are just starting
  to puff up.

5 Preheat the oven to Gas Mark 7/220°C/425°F.

6 Bake for 6–8 minutes until just cooked
  through. Transfer to a wire rack to cool.

Naan Bread

Makes: *6 breads* **Preparation time:** *25 minutes + proving + 10 minutes baking*
Freezing: *recommended*

Naan bread may be cooked in the oven or under a very hot grill.
Cooking in the oven creates a more uniform finish, without the
trademark blistering.

450 g (1 lb) strong white bread flour
2 teaspoons sugar
1 teaspoon salt
1½ teaspoons fast action dried yeast
1½ teaspoons black onion seeds
1 teaspoon baking powder
50 g (2 oz) butter, melted
175–200 ml (6–7 fl oz) warm semi-skimmed
  milk
150 ml (¼ pint) natural yogurt

1 Mix together the flour, sugar, salt, yeast, black
  onion seeds and baking powder. Make a well
  in the centre and add 25 g (1 oz) of the melted
  butter, the milk and yogurt. Combine to make
  a soft dough.

2 Turn out on to an unfloured work surface and
  knead (page 8) for about 10 minutes until
  smooth. Cover and prove (page 8) in a warm
  place until doubled in size. Grease two baking
  sheets.

3 Divide the dough into six. Using floured
  hands, form each piece into a 20 cm (8 inch)
  long teardrop shape that is thicker at the
  edges than in the centre. Place well apart on
  the baking sheets. Cover and prove for
  20 minutes, or until the dough is just
  beginning to puff up.

4 Preheat the oven to Gas Mark 7/220°C/425°F.

5 Bake the breads for 10 minutes. When
  they come out of the oven, brush with the
  remaining melted butter and either wrap in foil
  to keep warm or transfer to a cooling rack.

Variation: This makes a plain naan. If you
prefer something a little spicier, mix some
roasted and crushed coriander, fennel and
cumin seeds in with the flour.

Bagels

Makes: *8 bagels* **Preparation time:** *35 minutes + proving + 15 minutes baking*
Freezing: *recommended*

To achieve an authentic chewy texture, bagels must be dropped into boiling water for a minute before baking in the oven – thereby cooking them twice.

450 g (1 lb) strong white bread flour
3 tablespoons caster sugar
1½ teaspoons salt
1¼ teaspoons fast action dried yeast
300 ml (½ pint) warm water
For the glaze:
1 egg yolk
1 tablespoon water

1 Grease two baking sheets or line with baking parchment.

2 Place the flour, sugar, salt and yeast in a large bowl. Make a well in the centre and add the water. Mix to a soft dough.

3 Turn out on to an unfloured work surface and knead (page 8) for 8–10 minutes until smooth. Place in an oiled polythene bag and prove (page 8) in a warm place until doubled in size.

4 Knead the dough for a couple of minutes to even out any air bubbles. Divide the dough into eight and roll each piece out to about 25 cm (10 inches). Wet one end and press firmly together with the other to form a ring. Place well apart on the baking sheets, cover and prove for 30 minutes, until they are just over half their original size.

5 Preheat the oven to Gas Mark 6/200°C/400°F and bring a large pan of water to the boil.

6 Using a lightly floured slice, very carefully transfer one of the bagels to the boiling water. Simmer for 30 seconds before turning over. Simmer for a further 30 seconds, then remove with a slotted spoon. Drain well and set back on the baking sheet. Repeat with the remaining bagels.

7 Beat together the egg yolk and water and glaze each bagel. Bake for 15 minutes until golden. Cool on a wire rack.

Tips: If your pan is big enough, you can simmer two to three bagels at a time.

Try scattering seeds over the top before baking – linseed, poppy, sesame or black onion seeds all work well.

Pikelets

Makes: *around 26 pikelets* **Preparation time:** *10 minutes + proving + 30 minutes total cooking*
Freezing: *recommended*

These are great fun. Serve lightly toasted and buttered. Any left over will keep well for a couple of days or freeze beautifully.

225 g (8 oz) strong white bread flour
1 teaspoon caster sugar
½ teaspoon salt
1 teaspoon fast action dried yeast
¼ teaspoon bicarbonate of soda
175 ml (6 fl oz) warm semi-skimmed milk
175 ml (6 fl oz) hand-hot water
sunflower or vegetable oil, for brushing

1 Stir the flour, sugar, salt, yeast and bicarbonate of soda together in a mixing bowl. Gradually blend in the milk and water to make a smooth batter. Beat for a couple of minutes with a balloon whisk, cover with a clean, damp tea towel and leave in a warm place until the mixture becomes light and frothy. This may take up to 1½ hours.

2 Beat the batter again, this time for about 1 minute, until it is smooth.

3 Warm a large, non-stick frying pan over a medium heat. Brush the surface very lightly with oil. Carefully spoon a tablespoon of the batter into the pan to make a round. Depending on the size of your pan, you may be able to cook three or four spoonfuls at a time.

4 Cook the pikelets for about 2 minutes, until the bubbles have burst and the batter is almost set. Turn over and continue cooking for about 30 seconds until they are just starting to colour. The underside should be a light golden colour.

5 Repeat until all the batter has been used, greasing the pan lightly between batches. Cool on a wire rack.

Tip: This recipe can also be used to make crumpets. Cook 2 tablespoons of batter in greased 8 cm (3¼ inch) egg rings or biscuit cutters. The cooking time will be a little longer. Alternatively, downsize and make mini pikelets to use as a base for canapés.

Irish Soda Bread

Makes: *1 loaf* **Preparation time:** *15 minutes + 35–40 minutes baking*
Freezing: *not recommended*

This traditional Irish bread uses bicarbonate of soda rather than yeast. Plain flour is also used as, in the past, Ireland's wet climate meant that hard varieties of wheat could not be grown there.

225 g (8 oz) plain flour, plus extra for dusting
225 g (8 oz) plain wholemeal flour
1 tablespoon muscovado sugar
2 teaspoons bicarbonate of soda
1 teaspoon salt
50 g (2 oz) toasted pumpkin seeds
250 g (9 oz) carton buttermilk made up to
   300 ml (½ pint) with water
1 medium egg, beaten

1 Preheat the oven to Gas Mark 6/200°C/400°F. Lightly grease a baking sheet.

2 Mix together the flours, sugar, bicarbonate of soda, salt and pumpkin seeds in a large bowl. Make a well in the centre and add the watered buttermilk and egg. Stir to form a soft dough.

3 Turn out on to a lightly floured surface and work quickly and gently to just bring the mixture together into a ball. Place on the baking sheet and flatten slightly. Using a sharp knife, score a deep cross on to the bread.

4 Bake for 35–40 minutes until golden and the base sounds hollow when tapped.

American Pumpernickel

Makes: *1 loaf* **Preparation time:** *20 minutes + proving + 40–45 minutes baking*
Freezing: *recommended*

Traditional German pumpernickel bread is made from rye flour and rye berries using a sourdough starter. This recipe is the American version and produces a lighter loaf. The texture is more bread-like than the German version and is best left unsliced for a day to develop a more 'chewy' texture.

175 g (6 oz) strong white bread flour
80 g (3 oz) strong wholemeal bread flour
80 g (3 oz) wholemeal rye flour
1 teaspoon sugar
1 teaspoon salt
1½ teaspoons fast action dried yeast
2 tablespoons cocoa powder
1 teaspoon instant coffee powder
2 tablespoons molasses
1 tablespoon sunflower oil
225 ml (8 fl oz) hand-hot water
For the glaze:
1 egg white
1 teaspoon water

1 Combine the flours, sugar, salt, yeast, cocoa powder and coffee powder in a bowl. Make a well in the centre and add the molasses, oil and water. Mix to a soft dough.

2 Turn out on to an unfloured work surface and knead (page 8) for 5–6 minutes until smooth. Place in an oiled polythene bag and prove (page 8) in a warm place until doubled in size.

3 Grease a 900 g (2 lb) loaf tin.

4 Knock back (page 9) the dough and shape into an oblong by putting both hands under the piece of dough furthest away and bringing it towards you, folding it over the rest of the dough. Push down to seal the edge nearest you. Give the dough a quarter turn and repeat until you have a smooth-shaped oblong. Lay it in the prepared tin, seam side down, cover and prove until doubled in size.

5 Preheat the oven to Gas Mark 4/180°C/350°F.

6 Beat the egg white with the water and use to glaze the top of the loaf. Bake for 40–45 minutes. Cool on a wire rack.

English Muffins

Makes: *around 12 muffins* **Preparation time:** *30 minutes + proving + 12–15 minutes baking*
Freezing: *recommended*

These are a lovely standby to have in the freezer as they defrost
quickly and toast beautifully.

450 g (1 lb) strong white bread flour
50 g (2 oz) butter
2 teaspoons caster sugar
1 teaspoon salt
1 teaspoon fast action dried yeast
300 ml (½ pint) warm semi-skimmed milk
around 3 tablespoons fine semolina

1 Place the flour in a large mixing bowl and rub
   in the butter. Stir in the sugar, salt and yeast.
   Make a well in the centre, pour in the milk and
   mix to a soft dough.

2 Turn out on to an unfloured work surface and
   knead (page 8) for 8–10 minutes. Place in an
   oiled polythene bag and prove (page 8) in a
   warm place until doubled in size.

3 Grease four baking sheets and sprinkle them
   with the semolina.

4 Knock back (page 9) the dough and roll out to
   measure 1 cm (½ inch) thick. Using an
   8 cm (3¼ inch) plain round cutter, cut out
   11–12 muffins, re-rolling the dough as
   necessary. Space well apart on two of the
   prepared baking sheets, cover and prove in a
   warm place until doubled in size.

5 Preheat the oven to Gas Mark 7/220°C/425°F.

6 Carefully place a prepared baking sheet
   upside down on top of each tray of muffins.
   Bake for 12–15 minutes until golden. Cool on
   a wire rack.

Tips: The heavier the baking sheet on top of
the muffins, the flatter they will be. You may
need to shorten the baking time accordingly if
the muffins are considerably squashed!

Split these in half to make quick mini pizza
bases – spread with a little tomato purée
or ketchup, pile on some flaked tuna and
sweetcorn, finish with a little grated cheese
and grill until golden.

Ciabatta

Makes: *1 large loaf* **Preparation time:** *15 minutes + overnight + proving + 15–20 minutes baking*
Freezing: *recommended*

As this needs starting the day before, it is well worth making this large loaf, half of which may be frozen for another time. Choose very strong or premium bread flour for this recipe as it is a very wet dough.

**350 g (12 oz) very strong white bread flour,
plus extra for dusting
1 teaspoon salt
1 teaspoon yeast
3 tablespoons extra virgin olive oil
200 ml (7 fl oz) hand-hot water
For the starter batter:
115 g (4 oz) very strong white bread flour
1 teaspoon sugar
½ teaspoon fast action dried yeast
150 ml (¼ pint) hand-hot water**

1 Make the starter batter the night before. Place the flour, sugar and yeast in a small bowl and blend in the water. Mix to a smooth batter and cover with a damp tea towel.

2 The following day, mix together the flour, salt and yeast in a very large bowl. Make a well in the centre and add the starter batter, olive oil and a little of the water. Beat to a smooth paste, gradually adding all the water. You should end up with a thick batter. Cover with the damp tea towel and prove (page 8) for a couple of hours, until it almost triples in size.

3 Grease and flour a large baking sheet with sides.

4 Very carefully (so as not to knock out any of the air), tip the dough on to the baking sheet. Flour your hands well and pat and coax the dough into a long slipper shape, tucking the sides and ends under to plump up the dough. You should end up with a shape around 35 x 14 cm (14 x 5½ inches). Dust with what seems like an excessive amount of flour and prove, uncovered, for 45 minutes.

5 Preheat the oven to Gas Mark 7/220°C/425°F.

6 Bake for 15–20 minutes. Cool on a wire rack.

Olive and Feta Breads

Makes: *2 breads* **Preparation time:** *35 minutes + proving + 13–15 minutes baking*
Freezing: *recommended*

These delicious slipper breads make an ideal accompaniment to a main course salad in the summer.

350 g (12 oz) strong white bread flour
1 teaspoon caster sugar
1 teaspoon salt
1 teaspoon fast action dried yeast
1 teaspoon dried oregano
scant 225 ml (8 fl oz) hand-hot water (page 4)
3 tablespoons olive oil, plus 1 tablespoon for
   drizzling
50 g (2 oz) Feta cheese, cubed
25 g (1 oz) pitted black olives, roughly
   chopped

1 Combine the flour, sugar, salt, yeast and oregano in a mixing bowl. Make a well in the centre and add the water and 3 tablespoons olive oil. Mix together to form a dough.

2 Turn out on to an unfloured work surface and knead (page 8) for about 10 minutes until smooth. Work in the Feta cheese and olives. Divide the dough in two and place in an oiled polythene bag. Allow to rest for 10 minutes.

3 Grease a baking sheet.

4 Take one piece of dough and, using your hands, allow it to hang so that it takes on a teardrop shape measuring about 23 cm (9 inches) long and 13 cm (5 inches) in the widest part. The edges will be slightly thicker than the middle. Place on the baking sheet and repeat with the second piece of dough. Cover and prove (page 8) in a warm place until doubled in size.

5 Preheat the oven to Gas Mark 7/220°C/425°F.

6 Drizzle a little oil over the breads and bake for 13–15 minutes until golden. Cool on a wire rack.

Tip: Soft, black olives that have been preserved in salt are ideal for this recipe, even if it does mean going to the trouble of rinsing them and removing the stones.

Roasted Pepper Calzone

Makes: *6 calzone* **Preparation time:** *20 minutes + proving + 40–45 minutes cooking + 20–25 minutes baking* **Freezing:** *recommended*

Calzone are an Italian version of Cornish pasties. I have filled these with a medley of peppers – ideal for vegetarians.

350 g (12 oz) strong white bread flour, plus extra for dusting
¾ teaspoon fast action dried yeast
¾ teaspoon salt
2 tablespoons extra virgin olive oil
scant 250 ml (8 fl oz) hand-hot water (page 4)
For the filling:
1 red, 1 yellow and 1 orange pepper, de-seeded and sliced
400 g (14 oz) fresh tomatoes, halved
1 medium red onion, sliced
3–4 garlic cloves, unpeeled
2 sprigs of rosemary
3 tablespoons extra virgin olive oil
salt and freshly ground black pepper

1 Preheat the oven to Gas Mark 7/220°C/425°F.

2 Combine the flour, yeast and salt in a bowl. Make a well in the centre and pour in the oil and water. Mix to a soft dough.

3 Turn out on to an unfloured work surface. Knead (page 8) for about 10 minutes until smooth. Cover and prove (page 8) in a warm place until doubled in size.

4 Meanwhile, put the peppers, tomatoes, onion, garlic and rosemary into a large roasting pan so that they are in a single layer. Drizzle the oil over the top and season. Cook at the top of the oven for 40–45 minutes, turning half way through. Remove from the oven, cool and remove the skins from the garlic. Mash the flesh and mix into the roasted vegetables.

5 Grease two baking sheets and lightly dust with flour.

6 Divide the dough into six pieces. On a lightly floured surface, roll out each to an 18 cm (7 inch) circle. Place one sixth of the filling in the centre of each. Brush the edges with a little water. Turn over half of the dough to make a semi-circle and encase the filling. Pinch the edges together to seal, making a pattern as you wish. Place on the baking sheets, cover and prove for 30 minutes.

7 Bake for 20–25 minutes until golden. Serve warm or cold.

Garlic Butter Swirls

Makes: *12 rolls* **Preparation time:** *35 minutes + proving + 15–20 minutes baking*
Freezing: *recommended*

Serve these warm as an accompaniment to meatballs or spaghetti Bolognese, encouraging everyone to tear off a portion.

350 g (12 oz) mixed grain bread flour
25 g (1 oz) butter
¾ teaspoon salt
1 teaspoon fast action dried yeast
scant 250 ml (8 fl oz) hand-hot water (page 4)
For the garlic butter:
50 g (2 oz) butter, melted and cooled
2 garlic cloves, crushed
a squeeze of lemon juice
2 tablespoons chopped fresh parsley
salt and freshly ground black pepper

1 Lightly grease a shallow, 25 x 17 cm
   (10 x 6½ inch) baking tin.

2 Place the flour in a bowl and rub in the butter.
   Stir in the salt and yeast. Make a well in the
   centre and add enough water to make a soft
   dough.

3 Turn out on to an unfloured work surface and
   knead (page 8) for 8–10 minutes until smooth.
   Place in an oiled polythene bag for 10 minutes
   to give the dough a chance to relax.

4 Lightly flour the work surface and roll the
   dough out to 35 x 25 cm (14 x 10 inches). Mix
   together the butter, garlic and lemon juice and
   drizzle evenly over the dough, taking it right
   to the edges. Scatter the parsley over the top
   and season lightly.

5 Roll up the dough tightly from the long edge
   and pinch the seam together to seal. Using a
   sharp knife, cut the roll into 12 equal pieces.
   Turn the pieces so that the spiral is facing
   upwards and space evenly in the prepared
   tin. Pour any leftover garlic butter over the
   surface, cover and prove (page 8) in a warm
   place until doubled in size.

6 Preheat the oven to Gas Mark 7/220°C/425°F.

7 Bake the bread for 15–20 minutes until
   golden. Allow to cool slightly on a wire rack
   before serving warm.

Variation: Sprinkle a few chilli flakes over the
garlic butter before rolling up the dough.

Onion and Poppy Seed Bread

Makes: *1 loaf* **Preparation time:** *35 minutes + proving + 20–25 minutes baking*
Freezing: *recommended*

Rye flour gives this bread a lovely colour as well as adding to its flavour. This is a great loaf to take on a picnic and goes well with cheese.

3 tablespoons extra virgin olive oil
1 large onion, chopped
225 g (8 oz) strong white bread flour, plus
   extra for dusting
115 g (4 oz) wholemeal rye flour
1 teaspoon muscovado sugar
1 teaspoon salt
1 teaspoon fast action dried yeast
2 teaspoons poppy seeds
250 ml (8 fl oz) hand-hot water

1 Heat 1 tablespoon of the oil in a small pan and soften the onion for 5–10 minutes until golden. Cool.

2 Mix together the flours, sugar, salt, yeast and poppy seeds. Make a well in the centre and add the water and remaining oil. Mix to a soft dough.

3 Turn out on to an unfloured work surface and knead (page 8) for 10 minutes until smooth. Knead in the softened onion. Don't worry that the dough becomes wet and sticky at this stage – keep kneading until it becomes smooth again. Place in an oiled bag to relax for 10 minutes.

4 Preheat the oven to Gas Mark 7/220°C/425°F. Grease a baking sheet.

5 Lightly flour the work surface and roll out the dough to 28 x 18 cm (11 x 7 inches). Roll up from the long side and place on the baking sheet with the join on the bottom. Make random snips in the top using scissors, so that the bread has a spiky appearance. Cover and prove (page 8) in a warm place until doubled in size.

6 Bake for 20–25 minutes until golden and hollow when tapped on the base. Cool on a wire rack.

Mixed Seed Flower Pot Loaves

Makes: *2 loaves* **Preparation time:** *20 minutes + proving + 25–30 minutes baking*
Freezing: *recommended*

This method of baking recreates the clay ovens that used to be widely used and are still found in some parts of the world. The pots give the bread a lovely crust and provide a novel shaped loaf.

lard or white vegetable fat, for greasing
225 g (8 oz) strong wholemeal bread flour
225 g (8 oz) strong white bread flour
1 teaspoon salt
1¼ teaspoons fast action dried yeast
**8 tablespoons mixed seeds (sunflower,
    pumpkin, hemp and linseeds), toasted**
1 tablespoon sunflower oil
1 teaspoon runny honey
325 ml (11 fl oz) hand-hot water
For the topping:
**1 teaspoon salt, dissolved in 1 tablespoon
    boiling water, cooled**
sunflower seeds and linseeds, for sprinkling

1 'Season' two new 13 cm (5 inch) earthenware flower pots. Grease with lard or white vegetable fat and stand on a baking sheet. Bake in a hot oven for 5 minutes, then allow to cool. Repeat this process at least four times to ensure that you have a waterproof seal.

2 In a large bowl, combine the flours, salt, yeast and seeds. Make a well in the centre and add the oil, honey and water. Mix to a soft dough.

3 Turn out on to an unfloured work surface and knead (page 8) for 5 minutes until smooth. Divide the dough into two. Shape each piece into a round, and then elongate slightly so it

fits when placed in a flowerpot. Cover and prove (page 8) in a warm place until doubled in size and the dough is level with the top of the flowerpot.

4 Preheat the oven to Gas Mark 7/220°C/425°F.

5 Stand the flowerpots on a baking tray and brush with the salt water. Sprinkle liberally with seeds. Bake one rung below the centre of the oven for 25–30 minutes, covering with parchment paper if they brown too fast. Turn out on to a wire rack to cool.

Tips: Do take care when handling the pots as they will retain heat. Afterwards, clean them by wiping with a damp cloth – don't put them in water as this may break the waterproof seal you created.

If you do not wish to use flowerpots this quantity of dough is sufficient for two 450 g (1 lb) loaves, or one 900 g (2 lb) loaf. Alternatively, divide into 12 rolls.

Sage, Pancetta and Potato Bread

Makes: *1 loaf* **Preparation time:** *30 minutes + proving + 20 minutes simmering + 20–25 minutes baking* **Freezing:** *recommended*

This is delicious served warm from the oven with soups or casseroles.

175 g (6 oz) floury potatoes, peeled
350 g (12 oz) very strong white bread flour
¾ teaspoon salt
1½ teaspoons fast action dried yeast
freshly ground black pepper
175 ml (6 fl oz) hand-hot water
105 g (3½ oz) packet smoked pancetta slices, snipped
15 g (½ oz) fresh sage, chopped, plus 5 sage leaves to garnish
1 tablespoon extra virgin olive oil

1 Put the potatoes in a pan, cover with cold water, bring to the boil and simmer for 15–20 minutes until tender. Drain well and mash until smooth. Press a piece of clingfilm on to the surface of the mash to prevent it from drying and leave to cool slightly.

2 Combine the flour, salt and yeast in a mixing bowl. Season with pepper. Rub in the potato (which can be added while still warm). Make a well in the centre and add the water. Mix to a soft dough.

3 Turn out on to an unfloured work surface and knead (page 8) for 5–6 minutes until smooth. Oil a large mixing bowl, place the dough in it and cover with a damp tea towel. Prove (page 8) in a warm place until doubled in size.

4 Heat a small saucepan over a medium heat. Add the pancetta and cook for 2 minutes until it starts to crisp up and any fat runs out. Stir in the chopped sage and cook for a further 30 seconds. The pancetta should be very crisp. Set aside to cool.

5 Grease a baking sheet or 23 cm (9 inch) round sandwich cake tin.

6 Knead the pancetta, sage and any fat from the pan into the dough. For a rustic appearance, form roughly into a square or oblong and place on the baking sheet. Alternatively, shape into a ball and place in the prepared tin. Cover and prove until doubled in size. Preheat the oven to Gas Mark 7/220°C/425°F.

7 Dip each sage leaf in oil and arrange in a pattern on top of the loaf. Drizzle the remaining oil over the surface of the dough. Bake for 20–25 minutes until golden and the base sounds hollow when tapped. Cool on a wire rack.

Tip: If the dough is too sticky to handle, beat it with a wooden spoon instead of kneading and scrape the mixture into the tin.

Tomato and Red Pepper Tear 'n' Share Bread

Serves: *8–10* **Preparation time:** *30 minutes + proving + 25 minutes baking*
Freezing: *recommended*

Based on focaccia bread, this is similar to a vegetarian pizza but is best eaten as an accompaniment, rather than as a main meal.

350 g (12 oz) strong white bread flour
1 teaspoon sugar
¾ teaspoon salt
1 teaspoon fast action dried yeast
2 tablespoons extra virgin olive oil
225 ml (8 fl oz) hand-hot water
For the topping:
1 tablespoon sun-dried tomato paste
50 g (2 oz) small cherry tomatoes, halved
half a 290 g jar chargrilled red peppers in oil,
    drained and sliced
80 g (3 oz) mild, soft goat's cheese
50 g (2 oz) grated mozzarella
8 sprigs of fresh basil leaves
freshly ground black pepper
1 tablespoon extra virgin olive oil

1 Grease a 22 x 33 cm (8½ x 13 inch) Swiss roll tin.

2 Combine the flour, sugar, salt and yeast in a mixing bowl. Stir in the oil and water and mix to a soft dough.

3 Turn out on to an unfloured work surface and knead (page 8) for about 10 minutes until smooth. Leave to relax for 10 minutes. Press the dough evenly into the base of the prepared tin. Cover and prove (page 8) in a warm place until doubled in size.

4 Using your fingers, make dents all over the surface of the dough, pushing right through to the bottom of the tin. Gently spread the tomato paste over the surface. Push in the cherry tomatoes and scatter strips of peppers evenly over the top. Dot the goat's cheese over the dough in about ½ teaspoon measures and sprinkle with mozzarella. Scatter basil over the top and season with pepper. Finally, finish with a drizzle of olive oil. Leave to rise for a further 20–30 minutes.

5 Preheat the oven to Gas Mark 6/200°C/400°F.

6 Bake for about 25 minutes. Cool slightly before presenting at the table and inviting everyone to help themselves.

Tip: Always useful to have as a standby, it is just as quick to make up double the quantity of dough and freeze half. This can also be made in a 28 cm (11 inch) flan tin.

Fennel, Oregano and Pine Nut Ring

Makes: *1 loaf* **Preparation time:** *40 minutes + proving + 20–25 minutes baking*
Freezing: *recommended*

The fennel gives this bread a subtle flavour and keeps it moist. Like most home-made breads it is best eaten warm from the oven.

25 g (1 oz) butter
1 small fennel bulb, finely chopped
400 g (14 oz) strong white bread flour
50 g (2 oz) wholemeal rye flour, plus extra for dusting
1 tablespoon muscovado sugar
1 teaspoon salt
1½ teaspoons fast action dried yeast
2 teaspoons dried oregano
40 g (1½ oz) pine nuts, toasted
300 ml (½ pint) hand-hot water

1 Melt the butter in a pan, add the fennel and cook gently for about 10 minutes until softened but not browned. Leave to cool.

2 Meanwhile, mix together the flours, sugar, salt, yeast, oregano and pine nuts. Make a well in the centre and add the water. Stir to form a soft dough.

3 Turn out on to an unfloured work surface and knead (page 8) for 10 minutes until smooth. Gradually work in the cooked fennel. The dough will become sticky, so flour your hands if necessary. Place the dough in an oiled bag for 10 minutes to allow it to relax.

4 Grease a baking sheet.

5 Using your hands, shape the dough into a log and roll it until it is 50 cm (20 inches) long. Transfer to the prepared baking sheet and form it into a ring, sealing the ends together well. Make sure that the seam is underneath. Using a sharp pair of scissors, snip a pattern all around the top of the ring. Cover and prove (page 8) in a warm place until doubled in size.

6 Preheat the oven to Gas Mark 7/220°C/425°F.

7 Dust the bread with a little rye flour and bake for 20–25 minutes until golden. Cool on a wire rack.

Tip: This is a lovely bread for cheese sandwiches, or try it toasted the next day and spread with Marmite.

Beer Bread

Makes: *1 loaf* **Preparation time:** *15 minutes + proving + 20–25 minutes baking*
Freezing: *recommended*

It is always difficult to guess a dedicated beer drinker's reaction to bread made with beer. Will it be welcomed, or regarded as sacrilege? In fact the end product is quite subtle, producing a bread with universal appeal. It is great with a ploughman's lunch or if used to make sandwiches.

225 g (8 oz) strong white bread flour
115 g (4 oz) wholemeal rye flour, plus extra for
  dusting
¾ teaspoon salt
1 teaspoon fast action dried yeast
225 ml (8 fl oz) ale or stout
1 tablespoon sunflower oil
2 teaspoons runny honey

Tip: When you measure the beer, allow the frothy head to subside to ensure that you have the exact quantity needed.

1 Lightly grease a baking sheet.

2 Combine the flours, salt and yeast in a mixing bowl. Stir in the beer, oil and honey to make a soft dough.

3 Turn out on to a work surface and knead (page 8) for 7–8 minutes until smooth. Shape into a round, place on the baking sheet and, using a sharp knife, make five slashes across the top of the loaf. Cover and prove (page 8) in a warm place until doubled in size.

4 Preheat the oven to Gas Mark 6/200°C/400°F.

5 Dust the bread with a little rye flour and bake for 20–25 minutes. Cool on a wire rack.

Mushroom and Melted Cheese Pie

Serves: 6 **Preparation time:** *35 minutes + proving + 30 minutes baking*
Freezing: *recommended*

This is an unexpected pie, almost a ready-made cooked sandwich.

350 g (12 oz) strong white bread flour
1 teaspoon sugar
¾ teaspoon salt
1 teaspoon fast action dried yeast
2 tablespoons extra virgin olive oil
225 ml (8 fl oz) hand-hot water
a little oil for brushing
For the filling:
25 g (1 oz) butter
225 g (8 oz) flat field mushrooms, wiped,
    halved and thinly sliced
1 fat garlic clove, crushed
salt and freshly ground black pepper
115 g (4 oz) Fontina cheese, cubed
50 g (2 oz) grated mozzarella
2 teaspoons chopped fresh thyme
For the topping:
a few sprigs of fresh thyme
1 tablespoon extra virgin olive oil
coarse sea salt

1 Grease a 23 cm (9 inch) flan ring or loose bottomed sandwich tin.

2 Combine the flour, sugar, salt and yeast in a mixing bowl. Stir in the oil and water and mix to a soft dough.

3 Turn out on to an unfloured work surface and knead (page 8) for about 10 minutes until smooth. Cover and prove (page 8) in a warm place until doubled in size.

4 Meanwhile, melt the butter in a pan and sauté the mushrooms and garlic, continuing to cook until the juices have been reabsorbed by the mushrooms or have evaporated off. Season and leave to cool.

5 Halve the dough and press one half into the base of the prepared tin. Brush a little oil around the edge of the dough. Spoon the mushroom mixture evenly over the top to within 1 cm (½ inch) of the edge. Scatter the cheeses over the top and sprinkle with thyme. Take the remaining dough and roll out on a lightly floured surface to a 23 cm (9 inch) round. Place on top of the filling and press the edges down well to seal. The dough should completely cover the bottom layer.

6 With your fingertips, make random, deep indents all over the surface, pushing through to the filling without making any actual holes. Push sprigs of thyme into the dough and drizzle with the oil. Scatter a little sea salt over the top. Cover and prove for about 20 minutes, until the dough is puffy.

7 Preheat the oven to Gas Mark 6/200°C/400°F.

8 Place the pie on a baking sheet and bake for 30 minutes until golden. Leave in the tin for 5 minutes before removing and serving warm.

Variation: Pont L'Evêque and Taleggio cheeses melt beautifully and would work well instead of Fontina.

Brie and Redcurrant Bites

Makes: *24 rolls* **Preparation time:** *45 minutes + proving + 20–25 minutes baking*
Freezing: *recommended*

These are brilliant for a tear-and-share starter. Put them in the
centre of the table and invite your guests to help themselves.
They look especially pretty in the summer when thyme is young
and tender.

225 g (8 oz) strong white bread flour
25 g (1 oz) butter
½ teaspoon sugar
½ teaspoon salt
¾ teaspoon fast action dried yeast
150 ml (¼ pint) hand-hot water
For the filling:
2 tablespoons redcurrant jelly
**115 g (4 oz) Brie (not too ripe), cut into 24
   cubes**
2 tablespoons fresh thyme leaves
For the topping:
1 egg
1 tablespoon water
a handful of sesame seeds
fresh thyme leaves

1 Put the flour in a bowl and rub in the butter.
   Stir in the sugar, salt and yeast and mix to a
   soft dough with the water.

2 Turn out on to an unfloured work surface and
   knead (page 8) for 10 minutes until smooth.
   Place in an oiled polythene bag and leave to
   rest for 10 minutes.

3 Grease a 23 cm (9 inch) sandwich tin.

4 Divide the dough into 24 pieces. Working with
   one piece at a time while the others remain

covered, press out into a 6 cm (2½ inch)
disc using your fingertips. Place ¼ teaspoon
redcurrant jelly in the centre, followed by a
piece of Brie and a sprinkling of thyme leaves.
Bring up the edges of the dough to encase
the filling and pinch together to seal. Roll
gently in your hand to form a ball shape. Place
in the prepared tin.

5 Repeat with the remaining dough, placing
   the balls sealed side down in rings in the tin.
   Cover and prove (page 8) in a warm place
   until doubled in size.

6 Preheat the oven to Gas Mark 6/200°C/400°F.

7 Beat the egg and water together. Either brush
   the rolls with the egg glaze and sprinkle with
   sesame seeds, or just top each roll with some
   thyme leaves. Doing half and half takes longer
   but looks very attractive. Bake for 20–25
   minutes. Cool for 5 minutes then turn out on
   to a wire rack.

Tip: Serve these warm while the cheese is
still melted.

Golden Grain Finger Rolls

Makes: *16 rolls* **Preparation time:** *25 minutes + proving + 10–12 minutes baking*
Freezing: *recommended*

These rolls are tasty and sweet and have added texture from the grains and seeds. The egg gives them more of a 'cakey' texture.

450 g (1 lb) malted grain bread flour
50 g (2 oz) butter
1 tablespoon muscovado sugar
1 teaspoon salt
1½ teaspoons fast action dried yeast
25 g (1 oz) golden linseeds, toasted
25 g (1 oz) sunflower seeds, toasted
2 medium eggs, beaten
175 ml (6 fl oz) warm semi-skimmed milk
For the topping:
1 egg
1 tablespoon water
a handful of mixed linseeds and sunflower
    seeds

Tip: These are delicious filled or as an accompaniment to soup.

1 Lightly grease a baking sheet.

2 Put the flour in a bowl and rub in the butter. Stir in the sugar, salt, yeast and seeds. Add the eggs and milk and mix to a soft dough.

3 Turn out on to an unfloured work surface and knead (page 8) for about 10 minutes until smooth. Do not worry if the dough is quite sticky – keep working it and it will become more manageable. Divide the dough into 16 pieces, shape into sausages and place side by side, almost touching, on the baking sheet. Cover and prove (page 8) in a warm place until doubled in size.

4 Preheat the oven to Gas Mark 6/200°C/400°F.

5 Beat the egg and water together. Brush the rolls with the egg glaze and sprinkle with the seeds. Bake for 10–12 minutes. Cool on a wire rack.

Sweet Chestnut Bread

Makes: *2 batons* **Preparation time:** *20 minutes + proving + 25 minutes baking*
Freezing: *recommended*

If you don't know, it is hard to tell what ingredients have gone into this bread. The sweet chestnuts, enhanced with a little vanilla, produce a wonderful loaf that works well as a sweet or savoury accompaniment.

350 g (12 oz) strong white bread flour
115 g (4 oz) wholemeal rye flour
25 g (1 oz) butter
1 tablespoon sugar
1 teaspoon salt
1¼ teaspoons fast action dried yeast
100 g (3½ oz) vacuum-packed chestnuts,
 finely chopped
300 ml (½ pint) semi-skimmed milk
½ teaspoon vanilla essence

> **Tip:** Use leftover chestnuts to flavour any of the more basic breads in this book, such as Polenta Bread (page 30) or Soya Flour Bread (page 31).

1 Combine the flours in a bowl and rub in the butter. Stir in the sugar, salt, yeast and chestnuts. Add the milk and vanilla essence and mix to a soft dough.

2 Turn out on to an unfloured work surface and knead (page 8) for 8–10 minutes until smooth. Cover and prove (page 8) in a warm place until doubled in size.

3 Grease a large baking sheet.

4 Divide the dough in half and shape each piece into a baton about 30 cm (12 inches) long. Place well apart on the baking sheet and make diagonal cuts across the top of each. Cover and prove until doubled in size.

5 Preheat the oven to Gas Mark 6/200°C/400°F.

6 Bake for 25 minutes until golden. Cool on a wire rack.

Illustrated on page 33

Gruyère Baps

Makes: *8 giant baps* **Preparation time:** *30 minutes + proving + 15 minutes baking*
Freezing: *recommended*

These baps look enormous, but because the dough is so light they can afford to be huge. If you prefer, you can divide the dough into 12.

450 g (1 lb) strong white bread flour
50 g (2 oz) unsalted butter
1 teaspoon sugar
1 teaspoon salt
1½ teaspoons fast action dried yeast
2 medium eggs, beaten
175 ml (6 fl oz) warm semi-skimmed milk
200 g (7 oz) Gruyère cheese, finely grated
For the glaze:
1 egg
1 tablespoon water

1 Place the flour in a large mixing bowl and rub in the butter. Stir in the sugar, salt and yeast. Make a well in the centre and add the eggs and milk. Mix to a soft dough.

2 Turn out on to an unfloured work surface and knead (page 8) for 10 minutes until smooth. Place in an oiled polythene bag and leave in a warm place to prove (page 8) until doubled in size.

3 Lightly grease two baking sheets.

4 Knead most of the cheese into the dough, saving about 25 g (1 oz) for the top. Divide the dough into eight. Shape into rounds and hammer each one down hard with the heel of your hand to flatten. The baps should

measure about 10 cm (4 inches) across. Space well apart on the baking sheets, cover and prove until doubled in size.

5 Preheat the oven to Gas Mark 6/200°C/400°F.

6 Beat the egg and water together. Brush each bap twice with the egg glaze and sprinkle the remaining cheese over the tops. Bake for 15 minutes.

7 Remove from the oven and transfer to a cooling rack. Cover at once with a clean tea towel (this will give them a soft crust) and leave to cool.

Tip: These make a lovely lunchtime meal, filled with sliced ham, mustard and cress.

Chorizo and Tomato Bread

Makes: *1 loaf* **Preparation time:** *25 minutes + proving + 30–35 minutes baking*
Freezing: *recommended*

This bread is full of colour and flavour – vivid orange with a 'kick' from the chorizo. It is ideal as an accompaniment to a main course salad.

350 g (12 oz) strong white bread flour
2 teaspoons sugar
¾ teaspoon salt
¾ teaspoon fast action dried yeast
½ teaspoon dried thyme
1 tablespoon tomato purée
1 tablespoon olive oil
scant 225 ml (½ pint) hand-hot water (page 4)
50 g (2 oz) semi-dried tomatoes in olive oil,
**   roughly chopped**
40 g (1½ oz) thinly sliced chorizo, chopped

1 Combine the flour, sugar, salt, yeast and thyme in a bowl. Stir in the tomato purée, olive oil and enough water to make a soft dough.

2 Turn out on to an unfloured work surface and knead (page 8) for 8–10 minutes until smooth. Place in an oiled polythene bag and prove (page 8) in a warm place until doubled in size.

3 Grease a baking sheet.

4 Knead the tomatoes and chorizo into the dough. Form into a rugby ball shape, place on the baking sheet and, using a sharp knife, slash three times lengthwise along the top of the dough. Cover and prove until doubled in size.

5 Preheat the oven to Gas Mark 6/200°C/400°F.

6 Bake for 30–35 minutes. Remove to a wire rack and serve warm or cold.

Walnut and Raisin Bread

Makes: *1 loaf* **Preparation time:** *20 minutes + proving + 20–25 minutes baking*
Freezing: *recommended*

This bread is delicious topped with pears and cheese – try a soft, mild goat's cheese or a creamy blue such as Gorgonzola, dolcelatte or St. Agur.

175 g (6 oz) strong wholemeal bread flour
175 g (6 oz) strong white bread flour
115 g (4 oz) wholemeal rye flour, plus extra for
   dusting
1 teaspoon salt
1 teaspoon fast action dried yeast
115 g (4 oz) walnuts, toasted and chopped
80 g (3 oz) raisins
2 tablespoons walnut oil
1 tablespoon runny honey
325 ml (11 fl oz) hand-hot water

Tip: To toast the walnuts, fry them gently in a dry frying pan until they are golden brown.

Variation: Try substituting chopped dried apricots for the raisins.

1 Grease a baking sheet.

2 Combine the flours, salt, yeast, walnuts and raisins in a large mixing bowl. Stir in the oil, honey and water. Mix to a soft dough.

3 Turn out on to an unfloured work surface and knead (page 8) for 5–6 minutes until smooth. Shape into an 18 cm (7 inch) oblong, and place on the baking sheet. Using a sharp knife, make a cut along the length slightly to one side. Dust with a little rye flour. Cover and prove (page 8) in a warm place to double in size.

4 Preheat the oven to Gas Mark 6/200°C/400°F.

5 Bake for 20–25 minutes. Cool on a wire rack.

American Rye Bread

Makes: *1 loaf* **Preparation time:** *20 minutes + proving + 35–40 minutes baking*
Freezing: *recommended*

Traditional rye bread uses a sourdough starter to give it its distinctive taste. This American version takes a short cut, using natural yogurt instead to achieve a similar flavour.

300 g (10 oz) wholemeal rye flour
175 g (6 oz) strong white bread flour
1 tablespoon molasses sugar
1 teaspoon salt
1¼ teaspoons fast action dried yeast
200 ml (7 fl oz) hand-hot water
150 ml (5 fl oz) natural yogurt

1 Combine the flours, sugar, salt and yeast in a bowl. Make a well in the centre and add the water and yogurt. Mix to a soft dough.

2 Turn out on to an unfloured work surface and knead (page 8) for 5–6 minutes until smooth, scraping off the work surface as necessary. Place in an oiled bag and prove (page 8) in a warm place until doubled in size.

3 Grease a baking sheet.

4 Using floured hands, knock back (page 9) the dough and shape into a round. Place on the baking sheet and, using a sharp knife, make a deep cut down the centre. Cut three diagonal lines off this on each side to make a tree-like effect. Cover and prove once more until doubled in size.

5 Preheat the oven to Gas Mark 6/200°C/400°F.

6 Bake for 35–40 minutes, until golden and the base sounds hollow when tapped.

Tip: Rye flour handles differently to strong wheat flour. Just keep working the dough and don't be tempted to add extra flour, as you will end up with a dry loaf.

Sea Salt and Cracked Pepper Grissini

Makes: *24 grissini* **Preparation time:** *25 minutes + proving + 18–20 minutes baking*
Freezing: *recommended*

There are some wonderful sea salts available that are mixed with seaweed, spices, seeds and herbs, including their flowers. These all blend beautifully with this dough.

semolina, for sprinkling
350 g (12 oz) strong white bread flour
1 teaspoon sugar
1 teaspoon coarse sea salt
¾ teaspoon fast action dried yeast
1 teaspoon dried green peppercorns, lightly
  crushed
2 tablespoons extra virgin olive oil
scant 225 ml (8 fl oz) hand-hot water (page 4)
sunflower oil, for oiling

Tip: Delicious in the summer with a well-chilled aperitif, the dough could be made up without any flavourings, and then halved, and various ingredients added to each batch, such as sesame, fennel or poppy seeds. Alternatively, brush with garlic butter, or sprinkle with finely grated Parmesan.

1 Grease two baking sheets and sprinkle lightly with semolina.

2 Combine the flour, sugar, salt, yeast and peppercorns in a bowl. Make a well in the centre and add the olive oil and water. Mix to a soft dough.

3 Turn out on to an unfloured work surface and knead (page 8) for 10 minutes until smooth. Oil a patch of the work surface with sunflower oil, place the dough on it and cover with a tea towel. Leave to rest for 10 minutes.

4 Using a sharp knife, divide the dough into 24 pieces. Cover the pieces you are not working with. Using your fingers, and working from the middle outwards, roll out each piece into 28 cm (11 inch) lengths.

5 Place the breadsticks on the baking sheets, ensuring that they do not touch, and sprinkle lightly with semolina if you wish. Cover again and prove (page 8) in a warm place for 45 minutes.

6 Preheat the oven to Gas Mark 6/200°C/400°F.

7 Bake for 18–20 minutes until crisp and golden. Cool on a wire rack.

Onion Kuchen

Serves: 6–8 **Preparation time:** *35 minutes + proving + 30 minutes baking*
Freezing: *not recommended*

Kuchen means cake in German. Although most of the kuchen served in German coffee shops are sweet varieties, this is a savoury recipe.

225 g (8 oz) strong white bread flour
25 g (1 oz) butter
1 teaspoon caster sugar
½ teaspoon salt
¾ teaspoon fast action dried yeast
150–175 ml (5–6 fl oz) warm semi-skimmed
  milk
For the topping:
25 g (1 oz) butter
225 g (8 oz) onions, sliced
1 fat clove garlic, crushed
175 g (6 oz) mascarpone
salt and freshly ground black pepper
1 teaspoon poppy seeds

1 Grease a 20 cm (8 inch) sandwich tin.

2 Place the flour in a mixing bowl and rub in the butter. Stir in the sugar, salt and yeast and mix to a soft dough with the milk.

3 Turn out on to an unfloured work surface and knead (page 8) for about 10 minutes until smooth. Cover and leave to relax for 10 minutes.

4 Meanwhile, heat the butter in a fairly large saucepan. Add the onions and garlic and cook for about 10 minutes until softened but not coloured, stirring frequently. Turn out on to a plate and leave to cool.

5 Press the dough into the prepared tin, working it to the edges with your fingers and ensuring that it is an even thickness. Cover and prove (page 8) in a warm place until doubled in size.

6 Preheat the oven to Gas Mark 5/190°C/375°F.

7 Beat the mascarpone in a small bowl and stir in the onions and garlic until thoroughly combined. Season to taste. Spread the onion mixture evenly over the dough, leaving a 1 cm (½ inch) rim around the edge. Sprinkle with poppy seeds.

8 Bake for 30 minutes until the onion is tinged dark brown. Remove from the oven, run a knife around the edge of the tin and allow to stand for 10 minutes before transferring to a cooling rack. Serve warm.

Tip: Sprinkle with ⅛ teaspoon crushed dried chillies just prior to baking for an added kick.

Fiery Chicken and Pesto Pizzas

Makes: *2 pizzas* **Preparation time:** *35 minutes + proving + 30 minutes cooking +*
10–12 minutes baking **Freezing:** *not recommended*

These flavoursome pizzas are so much nicer than shop bought
ones. The chilli flakes add a little kick.

×2

225 g (8 oz) strong white bread flour
½ teaspoon salt
¾ teaspoon fast action dried yeast
1 tablespoon extra virgin olive oil, plus extra
 for brushing
150 ml (¼ pint) hand-hot water
semolina, for sprinkling
For the tomato sauce:
400 g can chopped tomatoes
1 garlic clove, crushed
1 tablespoon tomato purée
1 tablespoon extra virgin olive oil
½ teaspoon red wine vinegar
½ teaspoon dried oregano
sugar, salt and freshly ground black pepper, to
 taste
For the topping:
115 g (4 oz) cooked, diced chicken breast
 tossed in 2 teaspoons extra virgin olive oil
 and ⅛ teaspoon crushed chilli flakes
50 g (2 oz) buffalo mozzarella, torn into small
 pieces
4 teaspoons basil pesto
2 tablespoons grated Parmesan
a handful of fresh basil leaves

1 Combine the flour, salt and yeast in a bowl.
 Make a well in the centre and pour in the oil
 and water. Mix to a soft dough.

2 Turn out on to an unfloured work surface.
 Knead (page 8) for about 10 minutes until
 smooth, cover and prove (page 8) in a warm
 place until doubled in size.

3 Combine all the tomato sauce ingredients
 in a small saucepan. Bring to the boil and
 simmer, uncovered, for about 30 minutes, until
 thickened. Allow to cool.

4 Preheat the oven to Gas Mark 8/230°C/450°F.
 Grease two baking sheets and sprinkle them
 with semolina.

5 Divide the dough in two and roll out on a
 lightly floured surface to make two 25 cm
 (10 inch) discs. Place each on a baking sheet
 and brush lightly with olive oil.

6 Spread the tomato sauce to within 2.5 cm
 (1 inch) of the edge. Scatter over the chicken
 and mozzarella. Dot over the pesto and
 sprinkle with Parmesan.

7 Bake for 10–12 minutes until the base is crisp
 and the cheese has melted. Serve at once,
 sprinkled with fresh basil leaves.

Sesame Bread

Makes: *1 loaf* **Preparation time:** *20 minutes + proving + 15–20 minutes baking*
Freezing: *recommended*

The joy of this loaf is that it is actually formed from rolls that are joined together – built-in portion control! Using sesame oil in the dough brings out the flavour of the seeds and gives a deep underlying sesame taste.

350 g (12 oz) strong white bread flour
½ teaspoon sugar
¾ teaspoon salt
¾ teaspoon fast action dried yeast
1 tablespoon toasted sesame oil
225 ml (8 fl oz) hand-hot water
For the topping:
1 teaspoon salt dissolved in 1 tablespoon
  boiling water, cooled
1 tablespoon sesame seeds

1 Combine the flour, sugar, salt and yeast in a bowl. Add the sesame oil and water and mix to a soft dough.

2 Turn out on to an unfloured work surface and knead (page 8) for 8–10 minutes to a smooth dough. Cover and prove (page 8) in a warm place until doubled in size.

3 Grease a large baking sheet.

4 Without kneading the dough, cut into nine equal pieces. Place these on the baking sheet, offsetting the rolls, left and right, so that they touch and overlap the ones to each side by half. They will join up when proved to form an irregular shaped baton. Cover and prove in a warm place until doubled in size.

5 Preheat the oven to Gas Mark 7/220°C/425°F.

6 Brush the loaf with the salt water wash and sprinkle liberally with sesame seeds.

7 Bake for 15–20 minutes until golden. Cool on a wire rack.

Wild Herb Focaccia

Makes: *1 loaf* **Preparation time:** *25 minutes + proving + 20 minutes baking*
Freezing: *recommended*

You can use any herbs for this bread. Some are stronger than others, so vary the amount depending on which you choose.

350 g (12 oz) strong white bread flour
¾ teaspoon salt
¾ teaspoon fast action dried yeast
4 tablespoons extra virgin olive oil
scant 225 ml (8 fl oz) hand-hot water (page 4)
2 tablespoons chopped fresh herbs (such as thyme, rosemary or oregano)
¼ teaspoon coarse sea salt

1 Combine the flour, salt and yeast in a bowl. Make a well in the centre and add 2 tablespoons of the oil and the water. Mix to a soft dough.

2 Turn out on to an unfloured work surface and knead (page 8) for about 8–10 minutes until smooth. Allow to rest for 10 minutes.

3 Grease a 23 cm (9 inch) flan ring and place on a baking sheet.

4 Press the dough into the flan ring. Cover and prove (page 8) in a warm place until doubled in size.

5 Flour your fingertips and make indentations all over the surface of the dough. Push the herbs into the holes and drizzle with the remaining olive oil. Sprinkle with coarse sea salt, cover and leave to rise for another 20–30 minutes.

6 Preheat the oven to Gas Mark 7/220°C/425°F.

7 Bake for 20 minutes until golden. Transfer to a wire rack and serve warm or cold.

Stromboli

Serves: *8–10* **Preparation time:** *40 minutes + proving + 30–35 minutes baking*
Freezing: *not recommended*

This is an easy-cutting bread that creates ready-made sandwiches. Traditional Italian '00' flour makes a lovely smooth dough. Just remember to read the label and check that it is for bread making and contains at least 11 g protein per 100 g flour.

450 g (1 lb) strong white bread flour or '00'
    white flour
1 teaspoon salt
1 teaspoon fast action dried yeast
3 tablespoons extra virgin olive oil
300 ml (½ pint) hand-hot water
extra virgin olive oil, for brushing
For the filling:
75 g (2¾ oz) Parma, Prosciutto or Serrano
    ham
150 g (5 oz) mozzarella, torn
150 g (5 oz) Fontina cheese, cut into small
    cubes
25 g (1 oz) grated Parmesan
half a 280 g jar chargrilled artichoke hearts,
    cut into small pieces
half a 280 g jar chargrilled red peppers, thickly
    sliced
15 g (½ oz) fresh basil leaves
freshly ground black pepper

1 Combine the flour, salt and yeast in a large mixing bowl. Make a well in the centre and add the olive oil and water. Mix to a dough.

2 Turn out on to an unfloured work surface and knead (page 8) for about 10 minutes until smooth. Cover and prove (page 8) in a warm place until doubled in size.

3 Grease a baking sheet.

4 On a lightly floured work surface, roll out the dough to 40 x 28 cm (16 x 11 inches). Lay the ham over the surface to within 2 cm (¾ inch) of the edge. Scatter over the cheeses, artichoke hearts, peppers and basil leaves. Season with pepper.

5 Starting from the long edge, fold the third of the dough nearest to you over the filling, then fold the top third over. Place on the baking sheet, making sure that the join is underneath. Tuck the ends under, cover and prove for about 30 minutes.

6 Preheat the oven to Gas Mark 6/200°C/400°F.

7 Using a skewer, spike the dough randomly right through to the baking sheet. Brush the surface of the dough with olive oil and bake for 30–35 minutes until golden. Allow to cool slightly before serving warm or serve cold.

Variation: Alter the filling to suit your taste. Olives or semi-dried tomatoes would work equally well.

Pretzels

Makes: *12 pretzels* **Preparation time:** *30 minutes + proving + 15–20 minutes baking*
Freezing: *recommended*

Pretzels have a distinctive shape that might look complicated but is easy to create.

350 g (12 oz) strong white bread flour
½ teaspoon sugar
1 teaspoon salt
1 teaspoon fast action dried yeast
225 ml (8 fl oz) hand-hot water
For the topping:
1 egg yolk
1 tablespoon water
coarse sea salt

Variation: If you prefer a sweet version, omit the egg glaze and salt, lightly brush with water when they come out of the oven and toss them in a combination of ½ teaspoon cinnamon mixed with 4 teaspoons caster sugar.

Tip: You may need to lightly flour your hands when rolling out the strands if the dough is sticky.

1 Grease two baking sheets. Place the flour, sugar, salt and yeast in a large bowl. Make a well in the centre and add the water. Mix to a soft dough.

2 Turn out on to an unfloured work surface and knead (page 8) for 8–10 minutes until smooth. Place in a polythene bag and prove (page 8) in a warm place until doubled in size.

3 Knock back (page 9) the dough and divide into 12 pieces. Roll each out into a strand measuring 40 cm (16 inches). Take an end in either hand. Loop one end around, almost into a circle, so that the end just extends beyond the far side of the arc. Repeat with the other end to create a pretzel shape. Place on a baking sheet and repeat with the remaining stands. Cover and prove for about 30 minutes.

4 Preheat the oven to Gas Mark 6/200°C/400°F.

5 Beat the egg yolk and water together. Brush the pretzels with the egg glaze and sprinkle with a little sea salt. Bake for 15–20 minutes. Cool on a wire rack.

Pissaladière

Makes: *1 pizza* **Preparation time:** *50 minutes + proving + 20–25 minutes baking*
Freezing: *recommended*

This is a French version of pizza. It can be made with a bread or pastry base and with or without tomato. It has a strong flavour so only needs a green salad to accompany it.

225 g (8 oz) strong white bread flour
½ teaspoon salt
¾ teaspoon fast action dried yeast
2 tablespoons extra virgin olive oil
scant 150 ml (¼ pint) hand-hot water (page 4)
For the topping:
25 g (1 oz) butter
1 tablespoon extra virgin olive oil
450 g (1 lb) large Spanish onions, thinly sliced
2 garlic cloves, crushed
1 teaspoon sugar
1 tablespoon chopped fresh thyme
freshly ground black pepper
50 g (2 oz) can anchovy fillets, drained and
    halved lengthways
65–80 g (2½–3 oz) pitted black olives

1 Mix together the flour, salt and yeast. Make a well in the centre and add the oil and water. Mix to a soft dough.

2 Turn out on to an unfloured work surface and knead (page 8) for 8–10 minutes until smooth. Cover and allow to rest for 10 minutes.

3 Grease a 28 cm (11 inch) flan ring.

4 Press or roll out the dough and fit in the ring. Place on a baking sheet, cover and prove (page 8) in a warm place until doubled in size.

5 Preheat the oven to Gas Mark 7/220°C/425°F.

6 Heat the butter and oil in a large pan. Stir in the onions and cook over a low to medium heat for 15 minutes. Add the garlic and sugar, increase the heat and cook for a further 5 minutes, stirring occasionally, until golden. Remove from the heat and allow to cool. Stir in 2 teaspoons of the thyme and season with pepper.

7 Spread the topping over the dough. Arrange the anchovies over the top to form a lattice pattern. Stud each space with an olive.

8 Bake for 20–25 minutes. Serve warm.

Fougasse

Makes: *4 breads* **Preparation time:** *20 minutes + proving + 15–20 minutes baking*
Freezing: *recommended*

A flat bread from the Provence area of France, Fougasse has a distinctive leaf-shaped appearance and is similar to Focaccia (page 69). This is a plain version, but the dough may be flavoured to make sweet or savoury breads.

450 g (1 lb) strong white bread flour
1 teaspoon salt
1½ teaspoons fast action dried yeast
6 tablespoons extra virgin olive oil
scant 300 ml (½ pint) hand-hot water (page 4)
flour or semolina, for dusting

1 Combine the flour, salt and yeast in a large mixing bowl. Add 4 tablespoons of olive oil and the water. Mix to a soft dough.

2 Turn out on to an unfloured work surface and knead (page 8) for 8–10 minutes until smooth. Place in an oiled polythene bag and prove (page 8) in a warm place until doubled in size.

3 Grease two baking sheets and dust with flour or semolina.

4 Knock back (page 9) the dough and divide into four equal pieces. With your hands, or by rolling out on a lightly floured surface, shape these into 20 cm (8 inch) long and 13 cm (5 inch) wide ovals.

5 Make two short cuts down the centre of each bread, leaving a space between. Then make 3–4 diagonal cuts on either side, radiating almost from the middle, to give a leaf effect. Flour your finger and run it around each cut to enhance the slit and ensure that it does not close up when proved.

6 Place two fougasse on each baking sheet. Cover and leave to prove for just 30 minutes.

7 Preheat the oven to Gas Mark 7/220°C/425°F.

8 Drizzle the breads with the remaining oil and bake for 15–20 minutes until golden. Transfer to a wire rack to cool.

Tip: A craft blade works well for making clean cuts in the dough.

Apricot Loaf

Makes: *1 loaf* **Preparation time:** *25 minutes + overnight soaking + proving + 25 minutes baking*
Freezing: *recommended*

Soaking the apricots in Amaretto the night before gives them an added depth of flavour and soft chewiness. Use the partially rehydrated variety if you can.

150 g (5 oz) no-need-to-soak dried apricots,
   chopped
4 tablespoons Amaretto
225 g (8 oz) strong white bread flour
50 g (2 oz) strong wholemeal bread flour
50 g (2 oz) wholemeal rye flour
¾ teaspoon salt
1 teaspoon fast action dried yeast
scant 200 ml (7 fl oz) hand-hot water (page 4)

Tips: If you prefer your bread crusty, open the oven door for the final 5 minutes of cooking.

Try this as the base for bruschetta – sprinkled with a little olive oil, toasted in the oven and topped with mild goat's cheese and watercress.

1 Place the chopped apricots in a small bowl and pour over the Amaretto. Cover and leave overnight. Stir the next morning and then use when required.

2 Combine the flours in a mixing bowl and stir in the salt and yeast. Make a well in the centre and add the soaked apricots with any juices, plus the water. Mix to a soft dough.

3 Turn out on to an unfloured work surface and knead (page 8) for 8–10 minutes until smooth. You may need to flour your hands now and then as the apricot makes this dough quite sticky. Cover and prove (page 8) in a warm place until doubled in size.

4 Grease a baking sheet.

5 Knead the dough for a couple of minutes until smooth. Shape into an oblong and place on the baking sheet. Taking a sharp knife, make a deep slit lengthwise down the top and again just to one side. Cover and prove again until doubled in size.

6 Preheat the oven to Gas Mark 7/220°C/425°F.

7 Bake for 25 minutes. Cool on a wire rack.

Sugar and Spice

In many countries sweet breads are eaten in preference to biscuits and cakes. Germany has its Kaffé und Kuchen – coffee and cake – and France is renowned for its tantalising selection of patisseries. But there are many traditional English breads too, such as Sally Lunn or Bath Buns, and there is nothing more English than afternoon tea with a West Country split or toasted teacakes. As more ingredients are added, the distinction between bread and cake blurs, with some so rich or sweet they can double up as puddings.

Currant Buns, page 99

Danish Pastries

Makes: *16 pastries* **Preparation time:** *30 minutes + resting + proving + 15 minutes baking*
Freezing: *not recommended*

These taste and look spectacular! For a selection of pastries, divide the dough into four and use different fillings.

For the basic dough:
250 g (9 oz) butter, softened
450 g (1 lb) strong white bread flour
25 g (1 oz) caster sugar
1 teaspoon salt
1½ teaspoons fast action dried yeast
150 ml (¼ pint) semi-skimmed milk
2 medium eggs, beaten

1 Take the butter and place between two sheets of greaseproof paper, and then roll out into an oblong measuring 23 x 13 cm (9 x 5 inches). Chill to firm up while you make the dough

2 Combine the flour, sugar, salt and yeast in a mixing bowl. Make a well in the centre and add the milk and eggs. Mix to a soft dough. Turn out on to a work surface and knead (page 8) for 8–10 minutes until smooth. Cover and allow to rest for 10 minutes.

3 On a lightly floured work surface, roll out the dough into a 25 cm (10 inch) square. Place the butter in the middle and fold the long edges over to encase the butter, ensuring that they overlap. Press down to seal, making sure you also seal the ends.

4 Roll the dough into a strip measuring 40 x 18 cm (16 x 7 inches). Fold the top third down and the bottom third up to make an oblong. Press to seal. Place in a greased bag and refrigerate for 10 minutes. Repeat the rolling and folding process twice before using the dough to make one of pastries on pages 79–80.

Tips: Make the dough the night before and keep it in the fridge. It rolls out beautifully in the morning, and you can have freshly made pastries by coffee time!

When rolling out the dough, push the rolling pin down on the dough in short bursts to help distribute the butter before rolling out completely.

It is important that the baking sheet has a raised edge to catch any butter that comes out of the pastries during cooking.

Caramel Toffee Plaits

¼ quantity Danish Pastry basic dough
1 medium egg, beaten
2 tablespoons dulce de leche (caramel toffee)
25 g (1 oz) pecan nuts, chopped
For the glaze:
1 tablespoon sieved apricot jam
1 teaspoon boiling water

1 On a lightly floured surface, roll out the dough into a 25 x 20 cm (10 x 8 inch) oblong. Cut into four 13 x 10 cm (5 x 4 inch) rectangles and brush with beaten egg.

2 Spread 1½ teaspoons of caramel in a line down the length of one of the pieces of dough. Sprinkle an eighth of the nuts on top. Cut diagonal lines at 1 cm (½ inch) intervals, from the caramel to the edge of the dough. Fold alternate sides over the filling to make a plait, overlapping the dough in the centre. Repeat with the remaining dough.

3 Place on a greased baking sheet, brush with beaten egg and sprinkle with the remaining nuts. Allow to prove (page 8) slowly at room temperature for 20–30 minutes until slightly puffed up. Bake for about 15 minutes at Gas Mark 6/200°C/400°F

4 Remove to a cooling rack and brush with the apricot jam mixed with water while still warm.

Tutti Frutti Pinwheels

¼ quantity Danish Pastry basic dough
15 g (½ oz) butter, melted
1 tablespoon caster sugar
80 g (3 oz) dried tropical fruit, finely chopped
1 medium egg, beaten
For the glaze:
1 tablespoon sieved apricot jam
1 teaspoon boiling water

1 On a lightly floured surface, roll out the dough into a rectangle 30 x 13 cm (12 x 5 inches). Brush with melted butter, sprinkle with sugar and scatter the chopped dried fruit evenly over the top.

2 Roll up the dough, starting from the short edge, and seal well. Using a sharp knife, cut into four even-sized pieces. Place on a greased baking sheet and flatten down firmly with your hand so that each pastry is about 8–9 cm (3¼–3½ inches) in diameter. Brush with the beaten egg.

3 Allow to prove (page 8) slowly at room temperature for 20–30 minutes until slightly puffed up. Bake for about 15 minutes at Gas Mark 6/200°C/400°F.

4 Remove to a cooling rack and brush with apricot jam mixed with water.

Cherry Stars

¼ quantity Danish Pastry basic dough
1 medium egg, beaten
50 g (2 oz) stoned Morello cherries
  (from a jar or tin)
1 tablespoon no-added-sugar black
  cherry jam
For the icing:
50 g (2 oz) icing sugar, sifted
1½ teaspoons boiling water

1 On a lightly floured surface, roll out the dough
   into a 20 cm (8 inch) square. Divide into four
   equal pieces and brush with beaten egg.

2 Combine the cherries and jam and place
   a spoonful in the centre of each square of
   dough. Taking a sharp knife, make a cut from
   the cherries to each corner. Fold each corner
   to the middle, overlapping the cherries. Seal
   with beaten egg.

3 Allow to prove (page 8) slowly at room
   temperature for 20–30 minutes until slightly
   puffed up. Bake on greased baking sheets
   with raised edges for about 15 minutes at Gas
   Mark 6/200°C/400°F

4 Remove to a cooling rack. Mix together the
   icing sugar and water until smooth and drizzle
   over the warm pastries.

Apple Diamonds

1 medium cooking apple, peeled, cored and
  thinly sliced
1 tablespoon sultanas
1 tablespoon sugar
2 teaspoons water
large pinch of cinnamon
¼ quantity Danish Pastry basic dough
1 egg, beaten
For the glaze:
1 tablespoon sieved apricot jam
1 teaspoon boiling water

1 Place the apple, sultanas, sugar and water in
   a small pan and simmer until soft. Mash and
   stir in the cinnamon. Cool.

2 On a lightly floured surface roll out the
   dough into a 20 cm (8 inch) square. Cut into
   quarters. Cut along the pastry 1cm (½ inch)
   from the edge, leaving an uncut section at two
   opposite corners. Brush with beaten egg.

3 Place one quarter of the apple mixture in
   the centre of each square. Take one of the
   cut edges and fold it across to the opposite
   corner. Repeat with the other edge to form
   a diamond. Brush again with egg. Allow to
   prove (page 8) slowly at room temperature
   for 20–30 minutes until slightly puffed up.
   Bake on greased baking sheets with raised
   edges for about 15 minutes at Gas Mark
   6/200°C/400°F.

4 Remove to a cooling rack and brush with
   apricot jam mixed with water while still warm.

Chelsea Buns

Makes: *9 buns* **Preparation time:** *30 minutes + proving + 25 minutes baking*
Freezing: *recommended*

These buns make their own glaze – the butter and sugar combining to make a delicious, sticky butterscotch sauce at the bottom of the tin.

175 g (6 oz) strong white bread flour
25 g (1 oz) caster sugar
½ teaspoon salt
25 g (1 oz) unsalted butter, softened
1 medium egg, beaten
25 g (1 oz) unsalted butter, melted and cooled
 slightly
65 g (2½ oz) light muscovado sugar
115 g (4 oz) dried fruit and mixed peel
For the yeast batter:
1½ teaspoons dried yeast (not fast action)
½ teaspoon sugar
90 ml (3 fl oz) warm semi-skimmed milk
50 g (2 oz) strong white bread flour

1 First, make the yeast batter. Sprinkle the yeast and sugar over the milk and leave for 5 minutes. Stir in the flour to make a smooth batter and leave for another 15–20 minutes until frothy.

2 Combine the flour, sugar and salt in a mixing bowl. Make a well in the centre and add the softened butter, egg and yeast batter. Mix to make a soft dough.

3 Turn out on to an unfloured work surface and knead (page 8) until smooth. Cover and prove (page 8) in a warm place until doubled in size. Butter a shallow 18 cm (7 inch) square cake tin.

4 Lightly flour the work surface and roll out the dough, without knocking back, to 30 x 23 cm (12 x 9 inches). Pour the butter over the surface, spreading it evenly. (Do not worry that there are puddles, the sugar will soak these up.) Sprinkle the sugar on top, almost to the edges, followed by the dried fruit and mixed peel.

5 Roll up the dough tightly, starting from the long edge. Seal the edge well, making sure it is underneath the roll. Using a sharp knife, cut the dough into nine pinwheel buns. Place them cut side down in rows in the prepared tin. Cover and prove until the buns have joined up and the dough has doubled in size.

6 Preheat the oven to Gas Mark 6/200°C/400°F

7 Bake for 25 minutes (covering with a piece of foil or baking parchment after 10 minutes). Turn out onto a wire rack and serve warm.

Teacakes

Makes: *10 teacakes* **Preparation time:** *25 minutes + proving + 15 minutes baking*
Freezing: *recommended*

Split these generous-sized teacakes in half, toast and serve dripping with melted butter – delicious!

700 g (1½ lbs) strong white bread flour
50 g (2 oz) white vegetable fat
50 g (2 oz) caster sugar
1 teaspoon salt
1½ teaspoons fast action dried yeast
425 ml (¾ pint) warm semi-skimmed milk
80 g (3 oz) currants
25 g (1 oz) candied peel, finely chopped

1 Lightly grease two baking sheets.

2 Place the flour in a large mixing bowl and rub in the vegetable fat. Stir in the sugar, salt and yeast. Make a well in the centre, add the milk and mix to a soft dough.

3 Turn out on to an unfloured work surface and knead (page 8) for 10 minutes until smooth. Work in the currants and candied peel until evenly dispersed.

4 Divide the dough into 10 and shape into buns. Flatten these down firmly to 1 cm (½ inch) thick. Space the teacakes evenly on the baking sheets. Cover and prove (page 8) in a warm place until doubled in size.

5 Preheat the oven to Gas Mark 7/220°C/425°F

6 Bake the teacakes for about 15 minutes, or until they are golden and sound hollow when tapped on the base. Transfer to a wire rack to cool.

Sally Lunn

Makes: *1 loaf* **Preparation time:** *20 minutes + proving + 25 minutes baking*
Freezing: *recommended*

Sally Lunn is believed to have originated in Bath and is thought to be named after the French refugee who created the recipe. The loaf is traditionally split into three horizontally and filled with clotted cream and jam.

175 g (6 oz) strong white bread flour
25 g (1 oz) butter
25 g (1 oz) caster sugar
½ teaspoon salt
grated zest of 1 lemon
1 medium egg
For the starter batter:
2 teaspoons dried yeast (not fast action)
1 teaspoon caster sugar
175 ml (6 fl oz) warm semi-skimmed milk
50 g (2 oz) strong white bread flour
For the glaze:
1 tablespoon granulated sugar
1 tablespoon boiling water
1 tablespoon semi-skimmed milk

1 First, make the starter batter. Stir the yeast and sugar into the milk and beat in the flour. Do not worry that the mixture looks lumpy at this stage. Leave in a warm place for about 20 minutes until the mixture becomes frothy and smells yeasty.

2 Line a 15 cm (6 inch) round, loose-bottomed cake tin with a double thickness of baking parchment, ensuring it comes about 5 cm (2 inches) above the top of the tin.

3 Place the main quantity of flour in a bowl and rub in the butter. Stir in the sugar, salt and lemon zest. Beat the egg into the frothy yeast mixture. Tip this into the dry ingredients and, using a wooden spoon, beat for 1–2 minutes to give a smooth batter. Pour into the prepared tin and level the surface. Cover and prove (page 8) in a warm place until doubled in size. This can take 1½ hours.

4 Preheat the oven to Gas Mark 7/220°C/425°F.

5 Bake the bun one shelf below the centre of the oven for about 25 minutes, until set and golden.

6 While the loaf is baking, dissolve the sugar for the glaze in the boiling water and stir in the milk. Glaze the top of the bread as soon as it comes out of the oven. Leave to stand in the tin for 5 minutes before turning out on to a wire rack to cool.

Bath Buns

Makes: *7 buns* **Preparation time:** *30 minutes + proving + 15 minutes baking*
Freezing: *recommended*

These originate in Bath in Somerset and are based on a beaten batter rather than kneading. Mace, which used to be a popular spice, is traditionally used. Dried sour cherries make an interesting, tangy variation.

175 g (6 oz) strong white bread flour
25 g (1 oz) butter
40 g (1½ oz) caster sugar
½ teaspoon salt
¼ teaspoon ground mace
80 g (3 oz) sultanas or raisins
50 g (2 oz) sour cherries, roughly chopped
1 medium egg
For the starter batter:
2 teaspoons dried yeast (not fast action)
1 teaspoon caster sugar
150 ml (¼ pint) warm semi-skimmed milk
50 g (2 oz) strong white bread flour
For the glaze:
1 egg
1 tablespoon water
1 teaspoon caster sugar
coarsely crushed sugar cubes or sugar nibs

1 First, make the starter batter. Stir the yeast and sugar into the milk and beat in the flour. Do not worry that the mixture looks lumpy at this stage. Leave in a warm place for about 20 minutes until it produces a frothy head and smells yeasty.

2 Place the flour in a bowl and rub in the butter. Stir in the sugar, salt, mace and all the dried fruit. Beat the egg into the frothy yeast mixture. Tip into the dry ingredients and, using a wooden spoon, beat for 2–3 minutes to create a smooth batter. Cover and prove (page 8) in a warm place until doubled in size.

3 Grease two baking sheets. Preheat the oven to Gas Mark 6/200°C/400°F.

4 Beat the batter again, just for a minute, to knock out the air. Place seven large spoonfuls, spread well apart, on the baking sheets. Cover and prove.

5 Beat the egg, water and sugar together and glaze the buns. Sprinkle with a little crushed sugar. Bake for about 15 minutes, or until golden. Cool on a wire rack.

Saffron Flower Bread

Makes: *8 rolls* **Preparation time:** *20 minutes + proving + 15–20 minutes*
Freezing: *recommended*

Saffron has a unique flavour and an alluring colour. Something also happens to the texture of the dough when saffron is added, resulting in a soft roll that goes well with savoury Indian-style dishes or can be served as a sweet bun.

¼ teaspoon saffron strands
1 tablespoon boiling water
225 g (8 oz) strong white bread flour
25 g (1 oz) unsalted butter
25 g (1 oz) caster sugar
½ teaspoon salt
¾ teaspoon fast action dried yeast
50 g (2 oz) sultanas
150 ml (¼ pint) warm semi-skimmed milk
1 egg, beaten, to glaze

Tip: Baking the rolls together in a sandwich tin gives a flower-like appearance.

1 Crush the saffron strands in a pestle and mortar. Pour on the boiling water and leave the colour to seep out while you prepare the remaining ingredients.

2 Lightly grease a 20 cm (8 inch) round sandwich tin. Place the flour in a bowl and rub in the butter. Stir in the sugar, salt, yeast and sultanas. Make a well in the centre of the flour. Pour the milk on to the saffron liquid and stir to combine, then pour into the well. Mix to a soft dough.

3 Turn out on to an unfloured work surface and knead (page 8) for about 10 minutes until smooth. Divide the dough into eight even-sized pieces. Shape into rounds and space around the edge of the tin, with one round in the centre. Cover and prove (page 8) in a warm place until doubled in size.

4 Preheat the oven to Gas Mark 6/200°C/400°F

5 Brush the rolls with egg and bake for 15–20 minutes. Cool on a wire rack.

Croissants

Makes: *12 croissants* **Preparation time:** *35 minutes + relaxing + proving + 15–20 minutes baking*
Freezing: *recommended*

Croissants are not difficult to make but there are several stages of
rolling and folding. Choose a time when you have something else
to do and work the stages round it!

200 g (7 oz) unsalted butter, softened
450 g (1 lb) strong white bread flour
2 teaspoons sugar
¾ teaspoon salt
1½ teaspoons fast action dried yeast
1 medium egg, beaten
scant 225 ml (8 fl oz) hand-hot water (page 4)
For the glaze:
1 egg
1 tablespoon water

1 Place 175 g (6 oz) of the butter between two sheets of greaseproof paper. Roll out to a rectangle measuring 25 x 15 cm (10 x 6 inches). Refrigerate.

2 Place the flour in a mixing bowl and rub in the remaining butter. Stir in the sugar, salt and yeast. Add the egg and water and mix to a soft dough. Turn the dough out on to an unfloured work surface and knead (page 8) for about 10 minutes until smooth. Place in an oiled polythene bag and leave to relax for 10 minutes.

3 Flour the work surface and roll the dough out to measure 2.5 cm (1 inch) wider than the rolled butter. Take the butter from the fridge and place it in the centre of the dough. Fold the bottom third of the dough up, and the top third down. Press the edges down firmly with the rolling pin to seal. Repeat the rolling and folding, wrap the dough in greaseproof paper and chill for 10 minutes.

4 Repeat the rolling and folding process twice more, then chill for 20–30 minutes.

5 Repeat step 4. Grease two baking sheets with raised edges.

6 Flour the work surface again and roll out the dough into a rectangle measuring 46 x 30 cm (18 x 12 inches). Trim the edges and cut the dough into six squares. Cut each square in half diagonally to make 12 triangles.

7 Brush a little egg on one tip of the triangle. Roll the triangle up, starting from the opposite side. Place the croissant on the baking sheet, making sure that the egg-glazed tip is underneath the croissant to seal it. Curve the ends inwards to form a crescent shape. Repeat with the remaining triangles. Cover and prove (page 8) in a warm place for about 30 minutes until puffy. Preheat the oven to Gas Mark 7/220°C/425°F

8 Beat the egg and water together and brush the croissants with the glaze. Bake for 15–20 minutes, until golden. Cool slightly on a wire rack and serve warm.

Petit Pain au Chocolat

Makes: *18 petit pains* **Preparation time:** *35 minutes + relaxing + proving + 13–15 minutes baking*
Freezing: *recommended*

A variation on plain Croissants (opposite), these are delicious for a weekend treat.

200 g (7 oz) unsalted butter, softened
450 g (1 lb) strong white bread flour
1 tablespoon sugar
¾ teaspoon salt
1½ teaspoons fast action dried yeast
1 medium egg, beaten
scant 225 ml (8 fl oz) hand hot water (page 4)
175 g (6 oz) plain chocolate drops
1 egg, for brushing
For the glaze:
1 egg
1 tablespoon water

1 Follow the recipe for Croissants, steps 1–5 (opposite).

2 Flour the work surface again and roll out the dough into a rectangle measuring 46 x 30 cm (18 x 12 inches). Trim the edges and cut into three strips, each measuring 46 x 10 cm (18 x 4 inches).

3 Sprinkle one third of the chocolate drops down each strip of dough. Brush the dough with egg on either side of the chocolate, and fold the dough over to encase. Using the back of a heavy knife, push down on the dough 1 cm (½ inch) from the edge to seal thoroughly.

4 Cut each strip into six and place on the baking sheets. Cover and prove (page 8) in a warm place for about 30 minutes, until puffy. Preheat the oven to Gas Mark 7/220°C/425°F.

5 Beat the egg and water together and glaze the petit pains. Bake for about 13–15 minutes, until golden. Transfer to a wire rack and serve warm.

Doughnuts

Makes: *11 doughnuts* **Preparation time:** *30 minutes + proving + 15 minutes cooking*
Freezing: *not recommended*

These are absolutely scrummy!

450 g (1 lb) strong white bread flour
50 g (2 oz) unsalted butter
50 g (2 oz) caster sugar
1 teaspoon salt
1½ teaspoons fast action dried yeast
225 ml (8 fl oz) warm semi-skimmed milk
1 medium egg, beaten
½ teaspoon vanilla essence
5½ teaspoons stiff seedless red jam
vegetable or sunflower oil
caster sugar, for dusting

1 Grease two baking sheets well.

2 Place the flour in a large bowl and rub in the butter. Stir in the sugar, salt and yeast. Make a well in the centre and add the milk, egg and vanilla essence. Stir to make a soft dough.

3 Turn out on to an unfloured work surface and knead (page 8) until smooth. The dough will be quite wet and sticky but do not add any more flour. Keep working the dough with your fingertips until you end up with a smooth, silken ball. This will take 10–12 minutes.

4 Divide the dough into 11 pieces, form each piece into a ball and then flatten into a disc. Place half a teaspoon of jam in the centre of each, gather up the edges and pinch the dough to encase the jam. Carefully re-roll in the palm of your hand to make a ball. Place, well spaced, on the baking sheets, cover and prove (page 8) in a warm place until doubled in size.

5 Pour about 5 cm (2 inches) of cooking oil into a wide, heavy based pan. Heat until a cube of bread dropped into the oil browns in 30 seconds. Add 3–4 doughnuts and fry for 3 minutes, turning frequently until golden and puffy. Remove using a slotted spoon and drain on kitchen paper. While still warm, dust with caster sugar. Repeat with the remaining dough.

Variation: Try a chocolate and hazelnut spread filling or coating the doughnuts with a mixture of cinnamon and sugar.

Sugary Spice Dough Ball Ring

Serves: *8–10* **Preparation time:** *30 minutes + proving + 25 minutes baking*
Freezing: *not recommended*

This is a fun bread to share – simply pull off the individual pieces of dough! Adding cream cheese gives a lovely flavour and soft crumb.

350 g (12 oz) strong white bread flour
40 g (1½ oz) caster sugar
¾ teaspoon salt
1 teaspoon fast action dried yeast
80 g (3 oz) full fat cream cheese
150 ml (¼ pint) warm semi-skimmed milk
1 medium egg, beaten
For the topping:
50 g (2 oz) unsalted butter, melted and cooled
80 g (3 oz) caster sugar
1 teaspoon ground cinnamon

1 Combine the flour, sugar, salt and yeast in a bowl. Make a well in the centre and add the cream cheese, milk and egg. Mix to a soft dough.

2 Turn out on to an unfloured work surface and knead (page 8) for about 10 minutes, until smooth. The dough will be sticky, but persevere without adding any flour if you can. Flour your hands lightly and knead the dough into a smooth ball. Divide this into 24 little pieces. Shape into balls and place in an oiled polythene bag while you prepare the coating.

3 Pour the cooled butter into a small bowl. Combine the sugar and cinnamon in another bowl. Lightly grease a 1 litre (1¾ pint) ring tin. If you do not have a ring tin, use a 20 cm (8 inch) deep cake tin.

4 Take a couple of pieces of dough. Dunk them in the butter, then toss them in the cinnamon sugar to coat. Pop them randomly into the prepared tin (they will level themselves out on proving). Repeat with the remaining dough balls, then pour any remaining melted butter or sugary mixture over the top. Cover and prove (page 8) in a warm place until doubled in size. (The coating will crack slightly as it stretches.)

5 Preheat the oven to Gas Mark 6/200°C/400°F.

6 Place the ring mould on a baking sheet and bake for about 25 minutes, covering with a piece of greaseproof paper or foil after 10 minutes to prevent the top from browning too much. Turn out and cool on a wire rack.

Swiss Buns

Makes: *10 buns* **Preparation time:** *25 minutes + proving + 10–12 minutes baking*
Freezing: *recommended before icing*

These are a long established favourite in bakeries up and down the country.

450 g (1 lb) strong white bread flour
25 g (1 oz) butter
25 g (1 oz) caster sugar
1 teaspoon salt
1 teaspoon fast action dried yeast
300 ml (½ pint) warm semi-skimmed milk
For the icing:
350 g (12 oz) icing sugar, sifted
approximately 4 tablespoons hot water

Tip: Add a couple of drops of pink food colouring to the icing to make a pretty pastel pink alternative.

1 Lightly grease two baking sheets.

2 Place the flour in a large mixing bowl and rub in the butter. Stir in the sugar, salt and yeast and mix to a soft dough with the milk.

3 Turn out on to an unfloured work surface and knead (page 8) for about 10 minutes until smooth. Divide the dough into 10 pieces and shape into 15 cm (6 inch) sausage-shaped rolls. Place well apart on the baking sheets, cover and prove (page 8) in a warm place until doubled in size.

4 Preheat the oven to Gas Mark 7/220°C/425°F.

5 Bake the rolls for 10–12 minutes. Transfer to a wire rack, cover them with a clean tea towel (this softens the tops) and leave to cool.

6 To make the icing, put the icing sugar in a small bowl and gradually add enough hot water to make a fairly stiff paste. Spoon this along the top of each bun and leave to set.

West Country Splits

Makes: *6 splits* **Preparation time:** *30 minutes + proving + 12–14 minutes baking*
Freezing: *recommended before filling*

Also known as Cornish or Devonshire Splits, West Country splits are spread thickly with clotted cream and sandwiched with jam.

225 g (8 oz) strong white bread flour
25 g (1 oz) butter
1 rounded tablespoon caster sugar
½ teaspoon salt
¾ teaspoon fast action dried yeast
150 ml (¼ pint) warm semi-skimmed milk
For the filling:
clotted cream
strawberry conserve
sifted icing sugar, for dusting

1 Lightly grease a baking sheet.

2 Place the flour in a bowl and rub in the butter. Stir in the sugar, salt and yeast. Make a well in the centre, add the milk and mix to form a soft dough.

3 Turn out on to an unfloured work surface and knead (page 8) for about 10 minutes until smooth. Divide the dough into six pieces. Shape into rolls, place on the baking sheet and flatten with the heel of your hand to make baps about 8 cm (3¼ inches) across. Cover and prove (page 8) in a warm place until doubled in size.

4 Preheat the oven to Gas Mark 6/200°C/400°F

5 Bake the baps for 12–14 minutes until light and golden. Cool on a wire rack.

6 To serve, use a sharp knife to split open horizontally at an angle, leaving a hinge. Spread with clotted cream and spoon in some jam. Dust lightly with icing sugar.

Ginger Sultana Bun Loaf

Makes: *1 loaf* **Preparation time:** *30 minutes + proving + 35 minutes baking*
Freezing: *recommended before glazing*

This subtly flavoured milk bread is delicious on its own, lightly buttered, or toasted the next day and spread with honey.

450 g (1 lb) strong white bread flour
25 g (1 oz) butter
25 g (1 oz) muscovado sugar
1 teaspoon salt
1 teaspoon fast action dried yeast
300 ml (½ pint) warm semi-skimmed milk
80 g (3 oz) sultanas
40 g (1½ oz) stem ginger, finely chopped
finely grated zest of 1 orange
stem ginger syrup, to glaze

Variation: Try finely chopped dried pear instead of sultanas.

1 Grease a 900 g (2 lb) loaf tin.

2 Put the flour in a large mixing bowl and rub in the butter. Stir in the sugar, salt and yeast and mix to a soft dough with the milk.

3 Turn out on to an unfloured work surface and knead (page 8) for about 10 minutes until the dough is soft and smooth. Work the sultanas, chopped ginger and orange zest into the dough.

4 Shape and place in the prepared tin. Cover and prove (page 8) in a warm place until doubled in size.

5 Preheat the oven to Gas Mark 6/200°C/400°F.

6 Bake for about 35 minutes. Turn out on to a wire rack, brush with ginger syrup and leave to cool.

Malt Loaf

Makes: *1 loaf* **Preparation time:** *20 minutes + proving + 40–45 minutes baking*
Freezing: *recommended*

This bread does tend to take quite a while to prove as the malt inhibits its rising. It keeps very well for a few days.

225 g (8 oz) plain all purpose white flour
25 g (1 oz) muscovado sugar
½ teaspoon salt
¾ teaspoon fast action dried yeast
80 g (3 oz) sultanas
150 ml (¼ pint) warm semi-skimmed milk
2 tablespoons malt extract
1 tablespoon treacle
25 g (1 oz) butter, melted

Tip: This loaf has a natural matt appearance. For a shiny top, brush with clear, runny honey when you take the bread out of the oven.

1 Grease a 450 g (1 lb) loaf tin.

2 Combine the flour, sugar, salt, yeast and sultanas in a mixing bowl. Make a well in the centre and add the milk, malt extract, treacle and melted butter. With a wooden spoon, beat the mixture for a couple of minutes until smooth.

3 Pour the mixture into the prepared tin, cover and prove (page 8) in a warm place until it almost comes to the top of the tin. Preheat the oven to Gas Mark 6/200°C/400°F.

4 Bake the loaf for 40–45 minutes. Turn out and cool on a wire rack.

Trail Mix Loaf

Makes: *1 loaf* **Preparation time:** *20 minutes + proving + 30 minutes baking*
Freezing: *recommended*

Make sure you choose a luxury muesli for this recipe, packed with fruit, nuts and seeds.

175 g (6 oz) strong wholemeal bread flour
175 g (6 oz) strong white bread flour
115 g (4 oz) luxury muesli, plus extra for sprinkling
80 g (3 oz) mixed nuts, dried fruits and seeds
1 teaspoon salt
1½ teaspoons fast action dried yeast
2 tablespoons sunflower oil
2 tablespoons runny honey
250 ml (9 fl oz) warm semi-skimmed milk, plus a little extra to glaze

1 Grease a 900 g (2 lb) loaf tin.

2 Combine the two flours, muesli, mixed nuts, fruit and seeds, salt and yeast in a mixing bowl. Make a well in the centre and add the oil, honey and milk. Mix to a soft dough.

3 Turn out on to an unfloured work surface and knead (page 8) for 7–8 minutes until smooth. Shape into an oblong and place in the prepared tin. Brush with milk and sprinkle liberally with muesli. Cover and prove (page 8) in a warm place until doubled in size.

4 Preheat the oven to Gas Mark 7/220°C/425°F.

5 Bake on one shelf below the middle for 30 minutes. Turn out of the tin and cool on a wire rack.

Tips: Sprinkle the top of the dough liberally with the muesli. Any that falls to the bottom of the tin will stick to the edges as the dough rises, resulting in a lovely, tasty outer crust.

Try using rolled oats as a base for your own muesli: cranberries and pumpkin seeds provide colour, dates and dried apricots work well, roasted hazel and brazil nuts are delicious and linseeds, sunflower and sesame seeds add flavour and crunch.

Apple, Honey and Oat Buns

Makes: *12 buns* **Preparation time:** *25 minutes + proving + 12–15 minutes baking*
Freezing: *recommended*

My children loved these appley buns so much it was a surprise
any kept until the next day! These are delicious served warm.

350 g (12 oz) strong white bread flour
50 g (2 oz) medium oatmeal
¾ teaspoon salt
1 teaspoon fast action dried yeast
1 teaspoon mixed spice
40 g (1½ oz) dried apple rings, snipped
50 g (2 oz) sultanas
50 g (2 oz) butter, softened
2 tablespoons runny honey, plus extra to glaze
225 ml (8 fl oz) cloudy apple juice

Tips: Try topping these with glacé icing instead of the honey glaze.

These are baked in a muffin tray but could easily be shaped into rolls and cooked on a baking sheet.

1 Combine the flour, oatmeal, salt, yeast, mixed spice, snipped apple rings and sultanas in a bowl. Make a well in the centre and add the butter, honey and apple juice. Mix to a soft dough.

2 Turn out on to an unfloured work surface and knead (page 8) for about 10 minutes until smooth. Cover and prove (page 8) in a warm place until doubled in size.

3 Preheat the oven to Gas Mark 7/220°C/425°F. Grease the holes of a muffin tray.

4 Divide the dough into 12 pieces. Shape each into a ball and place in a hole of the prepared tray. Cover and prove until doubled in size.

5 Bake for 12–15 minutes until the buns are golden. Transfer to a cooling rack and brush at once with honey.

Currant Buns

Makes: *14 buns* **Preparation time:** *30 minutes + proving + 10–12 minutes baking*
Freezing: *Recommended before glazing*

These simple buns literally gleam once brushed with their sugary glaze, making them irresistible.

450 g (1 lb) strong white bread flour
25 g (1 oz) butter
25 g (1 oz) caster sugar
1 teaspoon salt
1 teaspoon fast action dried yeast
300 ml (½ pint) warm semi-skimmed milk
125 g (4 oz) currants
For the glaze:
1 tablespoon granulated sugar
1 tablespoon milk
1 tablespoon water

1 Lightly grease a baking sheet.

2 Place the flour in a large mixing bowl and rub in the butter. Stir in the sugar, salt and yeast and mix to a soft dough with the milk.

3 Turn out on to an unfloured work surface and knead (page 8) for about 10 minutes until smooth. Knead in the currants until evenly distributed.

4 Divide the dough into 14 pieces and shape into rolls. Place well apart on the baking sheet, cover and prove (page 8) in a warm place until doubled in size.

5 Preheat the oven to Gas Mark 7/220°C/425°F. Bake the buns for 10–12 minutes.

6 Prepare the sugar glaze by dissolving the sugar in the milk and water. Boil for 1 minute and then leave to cool. Transfer the buns to a wire rack and brush with the glaze while still hot. Allow to cool.

Illustrated on page 77

Lemon Brioche

Makes: *8 brioche* **Preparation time:** *40 minutes + proving + 15–20 minutes baking*
Freezing: *recommended*

Make these in individual fluted brioche tins, if you have them.

225 g (8 oz) strong white bread flour
25 g (1 oz) caster sugar
¼ teaspoon salt
grated zest of 1 lemon
50 g (2 oz) unsalted butter, softened
2 medium eggs, beaten
8 teaspoons luxury lemon curd
1 egg yolk, beaten
1 tablespoon water
For the yeast batter:
2 teaspoons dried yeast (not fast action)
1 teaspoon sugar
3 tablespoons warm semi-skimmed milk
25 g (1 oz) strong white bread flour

1 Make the yeast batter. Sprinkle the yeast and sugar over the milk and leave for 5 minutes. Stir in the flour to make a paste and leave in a warm place for 15–20 minutes until frothy.

2 Grease eight holes of a muffin tin or line each with a 13 cm (5 inch) square of baking parchment.

3 In a bowl, combine the flour, sugar, salt and lemon zest. Make a well in the centre and add the softened butter, eggs and yeast batter. Mix to a soft dough.

4 Turn out on to an unfloured work surface and knead (page 8) for about 10 minutes until smooth. Place in an oiled polythene bag and leave to prove (page 8) in a warm place until doubled in size.

5 Knead the dough. Cut off one quarter and place back in the oiled bag. Divide the remaining dough into eight pieces and flatten each into a disc in the palm of your hand. Place a teaspoon of lemon curd in the centre, pull up the edges and seal. Place, seam down, in the prepared muffin holes.

6 Divide the remaining dough into eight and roll each piece into a ball. Slightly elongate each to make a pear shape. Make an indent in the middle of each lemon curd-filled ball. Dip the pointed end of the small balls into the beaten egg yolk and press on top of the larger balls. Cover and prove again. Preheat the oven to Gas Mark 5/190°C/375°F.

7 Brush with the remaining egg yolk mixed with water and bake for 15–20 minutes. Cool on a wire rack.

Variation: For a chocolate brioche, use a cube of chocolate instead of the lemon curd or work chocolate drops into the dough itself.

Tip: This bread is more fragile than a standard loaf, so care needs to be taken when brushing with the glaze to ensure that air is not knocked out of the dough.

Swiss Mountain Buns

Makes: *20 buns* **Preparation time:** *30 minutes + proving + 10–12 minutes baking*
Freezing: *recommended*

Our eldest daughter Susie bought me a bar of Toblerone when I was writing this book, and so the idea for this recipe was born. The rest of the family are now keen to try out a variation using Mars Bars or Rolos!

450 g (1 lb) strong white bread flour
50 g (2 oz) unsalted butter
50 g (2 oz) caster sugar
1 teaspoon salt
1 teaspoon fast action dried yeast
300 ml (½ pint) warm semi-skimmed milk
200 g bar Toblerone
milk, for brushing
sifted icing sugar, for dusting

1 Place the flour in a large mixing bowl and rub in the butter. Stir in the sugar, salt and yeast and mix to a soft dough with the milk.

2 Turn out on to an unfloured work surface and knead (page 8) for about 10 minutes until smooth. Cover and prove (page 8) in a warm place until doubled in size.

3 Lightly grease two baking sheets.

4 Break the Toblerone into triangles and cut each triangle in half. Divide the dough into 20 pieces. Keeping the rest covered, take one piece of dough at a time and flatten to a disc in your hand. Place a piece of Toblerone in the centre and pinch up the edges to seal. Roll into a ball between the palms of your hands. Repeat with the remaining dough, placing the balls well apart on the baking sheets. Cover and prove again.

5 Preheat the oven to Gas Mark 6/200°C/400°F.

6 Lightly brush the buns with milk. Chop any remaining Toblerone and sprinkle over the tops. Bake for 10–12 minutes before removing and cooling on a wire rack. Dust thickly with icing sugar to resemble mountain peaks!

Tip: These buns are at their best while still warm as the chocolate will still be melted. Do take care not to burn yourself on the filling when you bite into them though.

Rocky Moon Buns

Makes: *16 buns* **Preparation time:** *30 minutes + proving + 10–12 minutes baking*
Freezing: *Recommended*

These buns were created after our daughter Beth watched Dr Who. They look quite startling but are a great way to encourage children to make their own bread, especially as no shaping is required.

450 g (1 lb) strong white bread flour
50 g (2 oz) unsalted butter
50 g (2 oz) caster sugar
1 teaspoon salt
1 teaspoon fast action dried yeast
300 ml (½ pint) warm semi-skimmed milk
115 g (4 oz) fudge, cut into small cubes
80 g (3 oz) chocolate-coated raisins or peanuts, Smarties, M&Ms or chocolate buttons
50 g (2 oz) coloured mini marshmallows

Tip: The basic dough is the same as for Swiss Mountain Buns, so why not make up a batch and split it to make half of each recipe.

1 Place the flour in a large mixing bowl and rub in the butter. Stir in the sugar, salt and yeast and mix to a soft dough with the milk.

2 Turn out on to an unfloured work surface and knead (page 8) for about 10 minutes until smooth. Cover and prove (page 8) in a warm place until doubled in size.

3 Either line two baking sheets with parchment paper (not greaseproof paper as the fudge and marshmallows will stick to it), or cut out 16 squares of paper and use these to line large muffin tins.

4 Work the fudge, sweets and marshmallows into the dough. Divide into 16 equal pieces and place just as they are on the baking sheets or in the muffin tins. Cover and prove again until doubled in size.

5 Preheat the oven to Gas Mark 6/200°C/400°F.

6 Bake the buns for 10–12 minutes. Cool on a wire rack.

Date and Orange Cake

Makes: *1 loaf* **Preparation time:** *15 minutes + proving + 45 minutes baking*
Freezing: *recommended*

This has more of a cake texture than bread and is made by beating the mixture rather than kneading.

175 g (6 oz) strong white bread flour
50 g (2 oz) unsalted butter
25 g (1 oz) light muscovado sugar
¼ teaspoon salt
¾ teaspoon fast action dried yeast
¼ teaspoon ground cinnamon
80 g (3 oz) plump dried dates, chopped
grated zest and juice of 1 orange
4 tablespoons warm semi-skimmed milk
1 medium egg, beaten
1–2 tablespoons chopped walnuts
2 teaspoons apricot jam, warmed

1 Grease and base line a 450 g (1 lb) loaf tin.

2 Place the flour in a bowl and rub in the butter. Stir in the sugar, salt, yeast, cinnamon and chopped dates. Make a well in the centre and add the orange zest and juice, milk and egg. Using a wooden spoon, beat well for about 2 minutes to give a smooth batter.

3 Pour the mixture into the prepared tin and level the surface. Cover and prove (page 8) in a warm place until the mixture has risen three quarters of the way up the tin. Preheat the oven to Gas Mark 6/200°C/400°F.

4 Sprinkle the walnuts over the top of the cake and bake for about 45 minutes. To see if the cake is cooked, insert a skewer into the centre. If it comes out clean, the cake is ready.

5 Remove the cake from the tin, brush with warmed jam and cool on a wire rack.

Swedish Tea Ring

Serves: *8* **Preparation time:** *40 minutes + proving + 15–20 minutes baking*
Freezing: *recommended before icing*

This variation on the traditional Swedish recipe contains orange.

225 g (8 oz) strong white bread flour
25 g (1 oz) unsalted butter
25 g (1 oz) caster sugar
½ teaspoon salt
1 teaspoon fast action dried yeast
grated zest of 1 orange
75 ml (3 fl oz) warm semi-skimmed milk
1 medium egg, beaten
50 g (2 oz) muscovado sugar
1½ teaspoons ground cinnamon
15 g (½ oz) unsalted butter, melted and cooled
For the icing:
80 g (3 oz) icing sugar
1 tablespoon orange juice
roughly grated zest of 1 orange

1 Lightly grease a baking sheet.

2 Place the flour in a bowl and rub in the butter. Stir in the sugar, salt, yeast and orange zest. Make a well in the centre, add the milk and egg and mix to a soft dough.

3 Turn out on to an unfloured work surface and knead (page 8) for about 10 minutes until smooth. Place in an oiled polythene bag and prove (page 8) in a warm place until doubled in size. Combine the sugar and cinnamon in a bowl.

4 On a lightly floured surface, roll out the dough to 38 x 23 cm (15 x 9 inches). Brush the melted butter over the surface, making sure that you go right to the edges. Spread the cinnamon sugar over the top to within 1 cm (½ inch) of the edge.

5 Roll the dough up tightly from the long edge, sealing the edge well. Place on the baking sheet, making sure that the join is underneath. Shape the dough into a ring and tuck the ends into each other.

6 Using sharp scissors, cut almost through to the middle of the dough at 4 cm (1½ inch) intervals. Take each section and twist firmly on to its side so that the cinnamon and sugar swirls are visible. Cover and prove again.

7 Preheat the oven to Gas Mark 6/200°C/400°F. Bake the ring for 15–20 minutes until golden, then cool on a wire rack.

8 Sieve the icing sugar into a bowl. Make a well in the centre and gradually stir in the orange juice. Drizzle over the top of the ring and scatter with orange zest to decorate.

Chocolate, Cherry and Coconut Cake

Makes: *1 cake* **Preparation time:** *35 minutes + proving + 20–25 minutes baking*
Freezing: *recommended*

Sharp dried cherries combine beautifully with dark chocolate and coconut to give a bread that is really more of a cake since it is finished with a thick drizzling of melted chocolate and dusted with icing sugar. This is lovely in the morning with coffee or for afternoon tea.

225 g (8 oz) strong white bread flour
25 g (1 oz) caster sugar
½ teaspoon salt
¾ teaspoon fast action dried yeast
50 g (2 oz) dried and sweetened sour cherries
25 g (1 oz) desiccated coconut
grated zest of ½ orange
1 medium egg, beaten
50 g (2 oz) creamed coconut dissolved in
    125 ml (4 fl oz) boiling water and cooled to
    hand-hot temperature
50 g (2 oz) good quality dark chocolate,
    roughly chopped
1 egg, beaten, to glaze
For decoration:
25 g (1 oz) dark chocolate, melted
sifted icing sugar, for dusting

1 Combine the flour, sugar, salt, yeast, cherries, desiccated coconut and orange zest in a mixing bowl. Make a well in the centre and add the egg and dissolved creamed coconut. Mix to a soft dough.

2 Turn out on to an unfloured work surface and knead (page 8) for 10 minutes until smooth. Cover and prove (page 8) in a warm place until doubled in size.

3 Lightly grease a baking sheet. Preheat the oven to Gas Mark 6/200°C/400°F.

4 Knead the chocolate into the dough until evenly incorporated. Leave to relax for 10 minutes before dividing the dough into two 35 cm (14 inch) strands. Join at one end with a little water if necessary, then plait or twist together. Tuck the ends under and place on the baking sheet. Glaze with beaten egg, cover and prove again.

5 Bake for 20–25 minutes. Cool on a wire rack. To decorate, drizzle the chocolate over the top of the bread and dust thickly with icing sugar.

Apricot and Almond Streusels

Makes: *8 streusels* **Preparation time:** *40 minutes + proving + 10–15 minutes baking*
Freezing: *not recommended*

Think of these tartlets as a simpler form of Danish pastries with a lower fat content. They are best eaten warm from the oven.

225 g (8 oz) strong white bread flour
25 g (1 oz) unsalted butter
25 g (1 oz) caster sugar
½ teaspoon salt
¾ teaspoon fast action dried yeast
6 tablespoons warm semi-skimmed milk
1 medium egg, beaten
¼ teaspoon vanilla essence
115 g (4 oz) white marzipan
410 g can apricot halves in syrup, drained, or 8
    fresh apricots, halved
1 egg, beaten, to glaze
sifted icing sugar, for dusting
For the topping:
1 tablespoon butter
2 tablespoons plain flour
1 tablespoon caster sugar
1 tablespoon flaked almonds
$^1/_8$ teaspoon ground cinnamon

1 Place the flour in a bowl and rub in the butter. Stir in the sugar, salt and yeast. Make a well in the centre, add the milk, egg and vanilla essence and mix to a soft dough.

2 Turn out on to an unfloured work surface and knead (page 8) for about 10 minutes, until smooth. Cover and prove (page 8) in a warm place until doubled in size. Grease two baking sheets.

3 For the topping, rub the butter into the flour and stir in the sugar, almonds and cinnamon.

4 Divide the dough into eight pieces and form into discs in your hands. Place well apart on the baking sheets and push out into 10 cm (4 inch) circles. Prick all over with a fork.

5 Divide the marzipan into eight and scatter pieces evenly over the circles. Put two apricot halves in the centre of each. Brush the edges with beaten egg and scatter over the topping. Cover and prove again until doubled in size. Preheat the oven to Gas Mark 6/200°C/400°F.

6 Bake the streusels for 10–15 minutes, then transfer to a wire rack. Dust with icing sugar and serve warm.

Tip: Substitute the apricots with plums for a change.

Blueberry Savarin

Makes: *1 savarin* **Preparation time:** *40 minutes + proving + 20 minutes baking*
Freezing: *not recommended*

Although savarins seem to have gone out of popularity, blueberries have never enjoyed such good press. This recipe combines the two to create a lovely summer pudding.

80 g (3 oz) unsalted butter
150 g (5 oz) strong white bread flour
1 tablespoon caster sugar
¼ teaspoon salt
50 g (2 oz) dried and sweetened blueberries
For the starter batter:
2 teaspoons dried yeast (not fast action)
1 teaspoon sugar
6 tablespoons warm semi-skimmed milk
25 g (1 oz) strong white bread flour
For the syrup:
80 g (3 oz) sugar
150 ml (¼ pint) water
2 tablespoons rum
1 tablespoon lemon juice
300 g (10½ oz) fresh blueberries

1 To make the starter batter, sprinkle the yeast and sugar on to the milk and leave for 5 minutes. Stir in the flour and put in a warm place for 20 minutes to froth. (Make sure you use a large enough bowl.)

2 Generously butter a 20 cm (8 inch) savarin tin and place on a baking tray.

3 In another bowl, rub the butter into the flour. Stir through the sugar, salt and dried blueberries. Make a well in the centre and gradually stir in the yeast batter. Beat for 2–3 minutes until smooth. Pour the mixture into the prepared tin, cover and prove (page 8) in a warm place for about 30 minutes, or until the batter almost reaches the top of the tin.

4 Meanwhile, make the syrup. Dissolve the sugar in the water, bring to the boil and simmer for 8–10 minutes until syrupy. Cool slightly before stirring in the rum and lemon juice and fresh blueberries. Preheat the oven to Gas Mark 6/200°C/400°F.

5 Bake the savarin for 20 minutes until golden and set. Cool slightly before running a knife around the edges. Leave to cool in the tin for another 10 minutes, then turn out on to a serving plate or tray.

6 While the savarin is still warm, prick it all over with a fork or skewer. Slowly pour over the syrup and blueberries and leave to soak in thoroughly.

Tips: This is actually better if made the day before so that the rum has a chance to soak right through the savarin.

Dried yeast works better in the starter batter than the fast action type.

Plum Custard Cake

Makes: *1 cake* **Preparation time:** *55 minutes + proving + 55 minutes baking*
Freezing: *not recommended*

This is definitely for comfort eating! Do not worry if the cake rises unevenly, it is part of the home-made appeal.

350 g (12 oz) strong white bread flour
40 g (1½ oz) unsalted butter
25 g (1 oz) caster sugar
½ teaspoon salt
1 teaspoon fast action dried yeast
1 medium egg, beaten
150–175 ml (5–6 fl oz) warm semi-skimmed
   milk
6 ripe plums, de-stoned and thinly sliced
80 g (3 oz) caster sugar
½ teaspoon ground cinnamon
sifted icing sugar, for dusting
For the custard:
600 ml (1 pint) semi-skimmed milk
½ teaspoon vanilla extract
115 g (4 oz) caster sugar
2 medium eggs, plus 2 egg yolks
25 g (1 oz) plain flour

1 Place the flour in a bowl and rub in the butter. Add the sugar, salt and yeast, then make a well in the centre and stir in the egg and milk to make a soft dough. Turn out on to an unfloured work surface and knead (page 8) for 10 minutes until smooth. Cover and prove (page 8) in a warm place until doubled in size.

2 For the custard, warm the milk and vanilla to just below boiling. Meanwhile, whisk the sugar and eggs until light and slightly thickened. Fold in the flour. Pour the hot milk on to the egg mixture, whisking all the time. Return to the pan and continue whisking until the mixture comes to the boil. Simmer for 1 minute before transferring to a bowl to cool. Cover with buttered paper to prevent a skin forming.

3 Line a 20 cm (8 inch) springform or loose bottomed cake tin with a double thickness of baking parchment, ensuring that it extends 10 cm (4 inches) above the rim of the tin.

4 Divide the dough into three. Using floured hands, press or roll out each piece into a 20 cm (8 inch) circle. Place one in the base of the prepared tin. Spoon a third of the cooled custard over the top. (It doesn't matter if this is still warm). Scatter one third of the sliced plums over. Combine the sugar and cinnamon and sprinkle one third of this over the plums. Repeat twice more.

5 Cover and prove for about 45 minutes, or until risen about 5 cm (2 inches) above the tin. Preheat the oven to Gas Mark 6/200°C/400°F.

6 Bake for 55 minutes or until risen and set. Do not worry if some of the plums become charred. Allow to cool in the tin for 15 minutes. Dust with icing sugar to serve.

Caramelised Apple Tart

Makes: *1 tart* **Preparation time:** *45 minutes + rolling + resting + proving + 25–30 minutes baking*
Freezing: *not recommended*

Serve this as a pudding, or warm it through and have with coffee.

225 g (8 oz) strong white bread flour
1 tablespoon sugar
¼ teaspoon salt
¾ teaspoon fast action dried yeast
25 g (1 oz) unsalted butter, softened
1 medium egg, beaten
90 ml (3 fl oz) warm semi-skimmed milk
115 g (4 oz) white marzipan
sifted icing sugar, for dusting
For the topping:
50 g (2 oz) unsalted butter
115 g (4 oz) caster sugar
6 dessert apples, peeled, cored and sliced into eighths

1 Combine the flour, sugar, salt and yeast in a mixing bowl. Make a well in the centre and add the butter, egg and milk. Mix to a soft dough.

2 Turn out on to an unfloured work surface and knead (page 8) for 8–10 minutes until smooth. Cover and allow to rest for 10 minutes.

3 On a lightly floured surface, roll the dough into a 28 x 18 cm (11 x 7 inches) rectangle. Roll out the marzipan to 13 x 10 cm (5 x 4 inches) and place in the middle of the dough. Fold each side of the dough over and seal by pressing down with the rolling pin. Roll out to roughly 30 x 13 cm (12 x 5 inches). Fold the top half down and the bottom up. Seal as before and repeat once more. Cover and leave to rest at room temperature for 10 minutes.

4 Repeat the rolling and folding twice, allow the dough to rest and then repeat twice more. Allow the dough to rest for a further 10 minutes.

5 Either roll out or push the dough into a greased 28 cm (11 inch) flan ring. Place this on a baking tray and cover. Leave to prove (page 8) in a warm place for 45 minutes.

6 Meanwhile, make the topping. Melt the butter in a pan large enough to take the apples in a single layer. Sprinkle on the sugar and then scatter the apples evenly over the top. Bubble over a medium heat for 20 minutes until golden. Cool. Preheat the oven to Gas Mark 6/200°C/400°F.

7 Use a fork to transfer apple slices on to the dough. Add a little of the syrup – too much will make the dough soggy. Bake for 25–30 minutes until golden. Allow to rest in the tin for 10 minutes before transferring to a wire rack. Serve warm, dusted with icing sugar.

Tip: Any leftover apple syrup makes a lovely sauce for bananas or ice cream.

Celebration Time

Bread making, with or without yeast, dates back centuries. Bread is found around the world and plays a part in many religions and faiths, often having a central role in cultural festivals and sacred rituals. Many of the recipes in this chapter are a labour of love, with great symbolic significance attached. They are often made only once a year, specifically for an important occasion or feast when the whole family gathers together.

Glacé Fruit and Nut Wreath, pages 124–125

Chollah

Makes: *1 loaf* **Preparation time:** *30 minutes + proving + 30 minutes baking*
Freezing: *recommended*

Chollah (or Challah) is a Jewish bread, traditionally eaten on the Sabbath. Made with milk, eggs, sugar and butter, it is quite rich. Any left-overs make a delicious bread and butter pudding.

350 g (12 oz) strong white bread flour
¾ teaspoon salt
40 g (1½ oz) unsalted butter
25 g (1 oz) sugar
1 teaspoon fast action dried yeast
2 medium eggs, beaten
125 ml (4 fl oz) warm semi-skimmed milk
1 egg, beaten, to glaze
½ teaspoon poppy seeds, for sprinkling

1 Place the flour and salt in a large mixing bowl and rub in the butter. Stir in the sugar and yeast. Make a well in the centre and add the beaten eggs and milk. Mix to a soft dough.

2 Turn out on to an unfloured surface and knead (page 8) for 10 minutes, until smooth. Place in an oiled polythene bag and leave in a warm place to prove (page 8) until doubled in size.

3 Lightly grease a baking sheet.

4 Divide the dough into three and, without knocking back, roll out using your fingertips into three strands, each measuring 35 cm (14 inches) long. Join the strands together at one end and seal with beaten egg. Plait the strands, seal with more beaten egg and place on the baking sheet. Tuck the ends under to plump up the shape, brush with beaten egg and cover. Leave in a warm place to prove until doubled in size.

5 Preheat the oven to Gas Mark 6/200°C/400°F.

6 Brush the plait again with beaten egg and sprinkle with poppy seeds. Bake one rung below the centre of the oven for 30 minutes. Cool on a wire rack.

Hot Cross Buns

Makes: *12 buns* **Preparation time:** *35 minutes + proving + 20 minutes baking*
Freezing: *recommended*

Traditionally eaten on Good Friday, these are best served toasted or warmed, split and buttered.

350 g (12 oz) strong white bread flour
50 g (2 oz) caster sugar
1 teaspoon salt
2 teaspoons mixed spice
1 teaspoon cinnamon
115 g (4 oz) currants, sultanas or raisins
50 g (2 oz) mixed peel
50 g (2 oz) unsalted butter, softened
1 medium egg, beaten
For the yeast batter:
1 tablespoon dried yeast (not fast action)
1 teaspoon sugar
225 ml (8 fl oz) warm semi-skimmed milk
115 g (4 oz) strong white bread flour
For the crosses:
4 tablespoons plain flour
3 tablespoons water
For the glaze:
2 tablespoons sugar
4 tablespoons semi-skimmed milk

1 First, make the yeast batter. Sprinkle the yeast and sugar on to the milk and leave for 5 minutes to let the yeast dissolve. Stir in the flour to make a paste. Place in a warm place for 15–20 minutes until frothy.

2 Combine the flour, sugar, salt, spices, fruit and peel in a large bowl. Make a well in the centre and add the butter, egg and yeast batter. Gradually draw in the dry ingredients and mix to a soft dough.

3 Turn out on to an unfloured surface and knead (page 8) for 8–10 minutes until smooth. Cover and leave to prove (page 8) in a warm place until doubled in size.

4 Grease a baking sheet.

5 Knock back (page 9) the dough. Divide into 12 equal pieces and roll each into a round. Arrange them in four well-spaced lines on the baking sheet. Cover and prove. Preheat the oven to Gas Mark 7/220°C/425°F.

6 Blend together the flour and water for the crosses to make a smooth paste. Spoon into an icing bag fitted with a small plain nozzle and pipe crosses on the buns.

7 Bake for 10 minutes, reduce the temperature to Gas Mark 5/190°C/375°F and bake for a further 8–10 minutes.

8 For the glaze, dissolve the sugar in the milk and simmer for 1 minute until syrupy. Leave to cool.

9 Remove the buns from the oven and, while still hot, brush with glaze to give a shiny finish. Transfer to a wire rack to cool.

Tsoureki (Greek Easter Bread)

Makes: *8 breads* **Preparation time:** *35 minutes + proving + 15–20 minutes baking*
Freezing: *recommended*

These Greek Easter breads are made from a plaited brioche-like dough. Traditionally, the eggs were dyed red to symbolise the blood of christ.

450 g (1 lb) strong white bread flour
2 tablespoons caster sugar
1 teaspoon salt
1½ teaspoons fast action dried yeast
grated zest of 1 orange
grated zest of 1 lemon
50 g (2 oz) unsalted butter, softened
2 medium eggs, beaten
150 ml (6 fl oz) warm semi-skimmed milk
8 medium eggs
For the topping:
1 egg yolk
1 tablespoon water
slivered almonds or sesame seeds, for
   sprinkling

1 Combine the flour, sugar, salt, yeast and orange and lemon zests in a large mixing bowl. Make a well in the centre and add the butter, beaten eggs and milk. Mix to a soft dough, gradually incorporating the dry ingredients.

2 Turn out on to an unfloured surface and knead (page 8) for 8–10 minutes until smooth. Place in an oiled polythene bag and leave to prove (page 8) in a warm place until doubled in size.

3 Grease two baking sheets.

4 Divide the dough into eight pieces. Take one piece, keeping the rest in the oiled bag to prevent it drying out. Cut this piece into three and, using your fingertips, roll out each third to 25 cm (10 inches). Plait these pieces together, joining the ends to form a ring. Transfer to a baking sheet and place an egg in the centre. Repeat with the remaining pieces of dough.

5 Cover both trays and prove until doubled in size. Preheat the oven to Gas Mark 6/ 200°C/400°F.

6 Beat the egg yolk with the water and brush the breads with the egg glaze, avoiding touching the eggs themselves. Sprinkle with slivered almonds or sesame seeds. Bake for 15–20 minutes until golden. Transfer to a cooling rack and serve warm or cold.

Tips: To avoid the eggs cracking, make sure that they are cushioned on the dough rather than being in direct contact with the baking sheet.

Pretty Cotswold blue eggs are used here, but you can use the more widely available brown speckled eggs and decorate them using non-toxic felt pens.

Irish Barmbrack

Makes: *1 loaf*
Preparation time: *overnight soaking + 40 minutes + proving + 55–60 minutes baking*
Freezing: *recommended*

This is a traditional Irish bread – barm meaning yeast and brack meaning bread. It is popular around Halloween and steeped in tradition. Various favours can be baked in the loaf, such as a gold ring. Superstition says that the lucky recipient will be married within a year.

400 g (14 oz) strong white bread flour
50 g (2 oz) caster sugar
½ teaspoon salt
1¼ teaspoons mixed spice
80 g (3 oz) butter, softened
1 medium egg, beaten
For the overnight soaking:
175 g (6 oz) raisins
175 g (6 oz) sultanas
115 g (4 oz) candied peel, cut small
600 ml (1 pint) strong, hot tea
For the yeast mixture:
1½ teaspoons dried yeast (not fast action)
1 teaspoon sugar
175 ml (6 fl oz) warm semi-skimmed milk
For the glaze:
1 egg
1 tablespoon water

1 The night before you want to make the bread, place the dried fruit in a bowl and pour over the tea. Stir, then cover with a tea towel and leave overnight to plump up the fruit. The following morning, strain the fruit through a sieve, pressing down gently with the back of a wooden spoon to remove as much excess moisture as possible.

2 Make the yeast mixture. Sprinkle the yeast and sugar on to the warm milk and stir. Leave in a warm place for 15–20 minutes until the mixture is frothy and the yeast has dissolved.

3 In a large mixing bowl, combine the flour, sugar, salt and spice. Make a well in the centre and add the softened butter, egg and yeast mixture. Mix to a soft dough. The mixture will probably be a little dry, so add a little of the soaked fruits to moisten if necessary.

4 Turn out on to an unfloured work surface and knead (page 8) for 6–8 minutes until smooth. The mixture will be sticky, but don't add any extra flour at this stage.

5 Gradually work in the soaked fruit, scraping the dough off the work surface as you go. It does become very sticky at this stage, so work quickly to incorporate all the fruit and then put the dough into a large oiled bowl. Cover and leave to prove (page 8) in a warm place. This will take up to 2 hours.

6 Line a 20 cm (8 inch) springform cake tin with baking parchment.

7 Beat the fruited dough mixture with a wooden spoon for 2–3 minutes, just to knock the air out. Spoon into the prepared tin and level the surface. Cover and prove again for 1½–2 hours.

8 Preheat the oven to Gas Mark 6/200°C/400°F.

9 Beat the egg with the water and use to brush the barmbrack. Bake for 55–60 minutes, covering the top with baking parchment after 15 minutes. Remove from the oven and leave in the tin for at least 15 minutes before turning out on to a wire rack to cool.

Tip: This is delicious thinly sliced and buttered.

Pulla

Makes: *1 loaf* **Preparation time:** *30 minutes + proving + 30–35 minutes baking*
Freezing: *recommended*

This is a speciality Finnish bread that is served as a braided strand or in a ring, as here.

350 g (12 oz) strong white bread flour
40 g (1½ oz) caster sugar
¾ teaspoons salt
1¼ teaspoons fast action dried yeast
1¼ teaspoons freshly crushed cardamom
  (about 28 pods)
grated zest of 1 orange
40 g (1½ oz) unsalted butter, softened
1 medium egg, beaten
175 ml (6 fl oz) warm semi-skimmed milk
For the glaze:
1 egg yolk
1 tablespoon water

1 Combine the flour, sugar, salt, yeast, crushed cardamons and orange zest in a bowl. Make a well in the centre and add the butter, egg and milk. Gradually incorporate the dry ingredients, mixing to a soft dough.

2 Turn out on to an unfloured work surface and knead (page 8) for about 10 minutes. This is quite a sticky dough, so keep going without adding any flour. Then, at the end, wash and dry your hands. Flour them and work the dough into a smooth ball. Place in an oiled bag and leave to prove (page 8) in a warm place until doubled in size.

3 Grease a baking sheet.

4 Without knocking back, cut the dough into three even pieces. Using your fingertips, roll these out into 50 cm (20 inch) strands and plait these together, linking the ends into each other to form a ring.

5 Place on the prepared baking sheet, cover and prove again.

6 Preheat the oven to Gas Mark 5/190°C/375°F.

7 Beat the egg yolk with the water and brush the ring with the egg glaze. Bake for 30–35 minutes, covering with baking parchment after 15–20 minutes if the loaf is browning too much. Transfer to a wire rack to cool.

Tip: Extracting cardamon seeds from their pods is rather a labour of love, but essential to the flavour of this bread. Probably the easiest way is to pound a few at a time in a pestle and mortar, just to break open the pods. Make sure all the green husks are removed and then crush the seeds to a coarse powder.

Mincemeat Plait

Makes: *1 plait* **Preparation time:** *30 minutes + proving + 25 minutes baking*
Freezing: *recommended prior to icing*

It is always useful to have something slightly different to produce at Christmas time. This plait makes a stunning alternative to mince pies. Make it in advance and freeze (minus the icing sugar), ready to warm up when needed.

225 g (8 oz) strong white bread flour
25 g (1 oz) butter
25 g (1 oz) caster sugar
½ teaspoon salt
¾ teaspoon fast action dried yeast
finely grated zest of 1 orange
1 medium egg, beaten
90 ml (3 fl oz) warm semi-skimmed milk
225 g (8 oz) good quality mincemeat
For the topping:
1 egg, beaten, for brushing
25 g (1 oz) flaked almonds
icing sugar, for dusting

1 Place the flour in a bowl and rub in the butter. Stir in the sugar, salt, yeast and orange zest. Make a well in the centre and add the egg and milk. Mix to a soft dough.

2 Turn out on to an unfloured work surface and knead (page 8) for about 10 minutes until smooth. Cover and leave to prove (page 8) in a warm place until doubled in size.

3 Grease a baking sheet.

4 Do not knock back the dough, but roll out to 30 x 23 cm (12 x 9 inches) on a lightly floured surface.

5 Spread the mincemeat down the centre of the dough in a band about 7 cm (3 inches) wide. Be sure to leave a gap of 2.5 cm (1 inch) at each end. Now take a sharp knife and make angled cuts on each side from the mincemeat to the edge at about 5 cm (2 inch) intervals. Brush the dough edges with egg and fold over the top and bottom pieces of dough on to the mincemeat band. Then, starting from the top, fold a strip from one side over the mincemeat, and then a strip from the other side. Repeat, making a plait shape, until all the strips have been incorporated.

6 Carefully transfer to the prepared baking sheet. Cover and prove.

7 Preheat the oven to Gas Mark 6/200°C/400°F.

8 Gently brush the plait with the beaten egg and scatter flaked almonds liberally over the top. Bake for 25 minutes, covering with a piece of parchment paper after 15 minutes.

9 Transfer to a cooling rack and serve warm, dusted with icing sugar.

Stollen

Makes: *1 loaf* **Preparation time:** *40 minutes + soaking overnight + proving + 30 minutes baking*
Freezing: *recommended*

Unlike most other home-made breads, Stollen tastes better if you leave it for a day or two before eating to allow the different flavours time to develop and fuse together. Stollen is a German bread, traditionally served at Christmas time.

50 g (2 oz) dried cranberries
50 g (2 oz) sultanas
25 g (1 oz) candied peel, chopped
3 tablespoons rum
225 g (8 oz) strong white bread flour
25 g (1 oz) unsalted butter
25 g (1 oz) caster sugar
½ teaspoon salt
1 teaspoon fast action dried yeast
40 g (1½ oz) pistachio nuts
grated zest of 1 lemon
6 tablespoons warm semi-skimmed milk
1 medium egg, beaten
15 g (½ oz) melted butter, for brushing
175 g (6 oz) white or gold marzipan
icing sugar, for dusting

1 Place the dried fruit and candied peel in a small bowl, pour over the rum, stir well, cover and leave to marinate overnight.

2 The next day, place the flour in a bowl and rub in the butter. Mix in the sugar, salt, yeast, pistachio nuts and lemon zest. Make a well in the centre and add the milk and egg. Mix to a soft dough.

3 Turn out on to an unfloured work surface and knead (page 8) for about 10 minutes until smooth. Strain any liquid off the marinated fruit and, using floured hands, knead the fruit into the dough. Place in an oiled polythene bag and prove (page 8) until doubled in size.

4 Grease a baking sheet. Using your hands, roll out the marzipan into a 23 cm (9 inch) sausage shape.

5 Lightly flour the work surface and, without knocking back the dough, roll it out to a 23 cm (9 inch) circle. Brush it all over with the melted butter and lay the marzipan down the centre. Fold both sides of the dough over to wrap up the marzipan and press down lightly to seal. Place on the baking sheet, cover and prove until doubled in size.

6 Preheat the oven to Gas Mark 6/200°C/400°F.

7 Brush the stollen with melted butter and bake for 30 minutes. Allow to cool on a wire rack before dusting thickly with sifted icing sugar.

Glacé Fruit and Nut Wreath

Makes: *1 wreath* **Preparation time:** *35 minutes + proving + 20 minutes baking*
Freezing: *recommended prior to icing*

This makes a lovely centrepiece at Christmas time. The nuts take on an almost praline-like flavour as they caramelise with the butter and sugar filling. The recipe list looks daunting, but it is really not as bad as it looks at first glance!

175 g (6 oz) strong white bread flour
25 g (1 oz) caster sugar
¼ teaspoon salt
25 g (1 oz) unsalted butter, softened
1 medium egg, beaten
For the starter batter:
1½ teaspoons dried yeast (not fast action)
½ teaspoon sugar
90 ml (3 fl oz) warm semi-skimmed milk
50 g (2 oz) strong white bread flour
For the filling:
50 g (2 oz) unsalted butter, softened
25 g (1 oz) ground almonds
25 g (1 oz) caster sugar
grated zest of 1 lemon
¼ teaspoon vanilla essence
115 g (4 oz) glacé cherries, chopped
50 g (2 oz) mixed peel
80 g (3 oz) mixed nuts (pecans, brazils,
   hazelnuts and flaked almonds), chopped
   and toasted
For the icing:
80 g (3 oz) icing sugar, sifted
1 tablespoon lemon juice

1 Begin by making the starter batter. Sprinkle the yeast and sugar over the milk. Leave for 5 minutes, then stir and mix in the flour. Leave in a warm place for 20 minutes or until the mixture is frothy.

2 In a bowl, combine the flour, sugar and salt. Make a well in the centre and add the butter, egg and starter batter. Stir these together, gradually incorporating the dry ingredients until you have a soft dough.

3 Turn out on to an unfloured work surface and knead (page 8) for about 10 minutes until smooth. Place in an oiled polythene bag and leave to prove (page 8) in a warm place until doubled in size.

4 Meanwhile, make the filling. Beat together the butter, ground almonds, sugar, lemon zest and vanilla essence to a smooth paste. Then work in the cherries and mixed peel. Grease a large baking tray.

5 Without knocking the dough back, tip it out on to a floured surface. Roll out into a 30 x 23 cm (12 x 9 inches) rectangle. Spread the filling mixture over the entire surface – almost to the edges – and scatter the chopped and toasted nuts evenly over the top.

6 Roll the dough up tightly from the long edge and pinch together to seal. Remove any trace of flour from the work surface and, using your fingers, roll out the dough into a sausage shape, keeping going until it measures 60 cm (24 inches) in length.

7 Take a sharp knife and cut through the middle of the sausage down the entire length. Turn the two pieces so that the filling is facing upwards. Place one end of each strand on the baking tray, and then plait the pieces together, bending them round in a circle. Weave in the ends to form a perfect ring. Cover and prove until doubled in size. Preheat the oven to Gas Mark 6/200°C/400°F.

8 Bake the ring for 20 minutes, covering half way through with baking parchment if it is browning too much. Transfer to a wire rack to cool.

9 In a small bowl, blend the icing sugar to a smooth paste with the lemon juice. Drizzle over the wreath.

Tip: Nuts brown best in the oven. They'll only take 5–10 minutes at a medium temperature, but do keep an eye on them as they can easily burn.

Illustrated on page 113

Panettone

Makes: *1 loaf* **Preparation time:** *25 minutes + proving + 35–45 minutes baking*
Freezing: *recommended*

An Italian bread, traditionally made at Christmas time, Panettone has a distinctive shape. Since it is rich in eggs, sugar and butter, it will take longer to prove than other breads, so don't be tempted to bake it before it has fully risen. Any leftovers make a wonderful base for bread and butter pudding.

400 g (14 oz) strong white bread flour
50 g (2 oz) caster sugar
½ teaspoon salt
1½ teaspoons fast action dried yeast
finely grated zest of 1 lemon
80 g (3 oz) raisins
80 g (3 oz) candied peel, fined chopped
80g (3 oz) unsalted butter, melted, plus extra
  for brushing
2 medium eggs, beaten
125 ml (4 fl oz) warm semi-skimmed milk
1 teaspoon vanilla extract

1 Combine the flour, sugar, salt, yeast and lemon zest in a bowl. Stir in the raisins and candied peel. Make a well in the centre and add the butter, eggs, milk and vanilla extract. Mix to a soft dough.

2 Turn out on to an unfloured work surface and knead (page 8) for 10 minutes until smooth. Cover and leave to prove (page 8) in a warm place until doubled in size. (This could take about 2 hours.)

3 Line a 15 cm (6 inch) spring clip or loose bottomed cake tin with a double thickness of baking parchment. Make sure that the paper is 5 cm (2 inches) higher than the tin.

4 Knead the dough again and form into a round. Place in the tin, cover and leave to prove until the dough rises almost to the top of the lining paper (about 1½ hours).

5 Preheat the oven to Gas Mark 6/200°C/400°F. Set the shelf to one rung below the middle.

6 Bake for 35–45 minutes, covering with buttered paper after 15 minutes to prevent it from over browning.

7 Leave the Panettone in the tin for 5–10 minutes before turning out on to a wire rack to cool. The base should sound hollow when tapped. Brush the top with melted butter while still warm.

Tip: Dust the Panettone with sifted icing sugar to give it a Christmasy feel!

Scandinavian Julekage

Makes: *1 loaf* **Preparation time:** *30 minutes + proving + 35–45 minutes baking*
Freezing: *recommended*

Julekage is traditionally served in Scandinavian countries at Christmas. Candied fruit, such as cherries and pineapple, are incorporated into a dough enriched with butter and eggs to give brightly coloured 'jewels' of red, orange and yellow.

450 g (1 lb) strong white bread flour
50 g (2 oz) caster sugar
¾ teaspoon salt
1½ teaspoons fast action dried yeast
½ teaspoon freshly ground cardamom (seeds from 13–14 pods)
grated zest of 1 lemon
115 g (4 oz) dried sweetened tropical fruit (pineapple, papaya, mango and melon)
50 g (2 oz) glacé cherries, roughly chopped
50 g (2 oz) mixed peel
80 g (3 oz) unsalted butter, melted
2 medium eggs, beaten
150 ml (¼ pint) warm semi-skimmed milk
For the icing:
50 g (2 oz) icing sugar
2½ teaspoons boiling water

1 Combine the flour, sugar, salt, yeast, cardamon and lemon zest in a bowl. Stir in the tropical fruit, cherries and mixed peel and make a well in the centre. Add the butter, eggs and milk and mix to a soft dough.

2 Turn out on to an unfloured work surface and knead (page 8) for 10 minutes until smooth. Cover and leave to prove (page 8) in a warm place until doubled in size.

3 Line a 20 cm (8 inch) spring clip cake tin with a double thickness of baking parchment so that it extends 5 cm (2 inches) beyond the rim.

4 Knead the dough again and form into a round. Place in the tin, cover and prove until the dough expands to fill the tin and almost reaches the top.

5 Preheat the oven to Gas Mark 6/200°C/400°F.

6 Bake for 35–45 minutes, covering with buttered paper after 15 minutes to prevent it from over browning.

7 Leave in the tin for 5–10 minutes before turning out on to a wire rack. The bottom should sound hollow when tapped.

8 While the bread is still warm, blend the icing sugar and water together. Drizzle the icing backwards and forwards across the top of the bread to decorate.

Tip: This bread will take a long time to prove, up to 2 hours for the first rising and almost as long for the second. Be patient as it is well worth the result. Because of the added butter it keeps for longer than most breads.

Yeast Free, Gluten Free or Wheat Free

For those who are unable to tolerate the main ingredients in bread – notably wheat, the gluten found in it and yeast – this chapter offers some alternative suggestions. Wheat and gluten free flour is available. It is made up of a variety of different flours blended in a combination to ensure an end product that balances the various attributes of each, whether it is valued for its colour, flavour or water absorbency. Typical flours that might be used include tapioca, potato and rice, together with a gluten improver.

Peshwari Mini Naans, page 140

Cornbread with Parmesan and Sun-dried Tomatoes

Serves: 8 **Preparation time:** *20 minutes + 20–25 minutes baking*
Freezing: *recommended*

Rustle up this delicious bread in no time at all and serve warm from the oven as an ideal accompaniment to soup or a casserole. Cornbread is best eaten fresh on the day it is made. If the bread has been frozen, defrost, wrap in foil and reheat before serving.

150 g (5 oz) cornmeal or polenta
150 g (5 oz) plain flour
1 tablespoon baking powder
1 tablespoon caster sugar
½ teaspoon salt
50 g (2 oz) Parmesan, grated
15 g (½ oz) fresh basil leaves, torn
generous grinding of black pepper
250 g carton buttermilk
80 g (3 oz) drained semi-dried tomatoes in oil, snipped
2 medium eggs, beaten
2 tablespoons extra virgin olive oil

1 Grease and base line a shallow baking tin measuring 25 x 15 cm (10 x 6 inches). Preheat the oven to Gas Mark 6/200°C/400°F.

2 In a large bowl, combine the cornmeal, flour, baking powder, sugar and salt. Stir in the Parmesan and basil leaves and season with pepper.

3 Make a well in the centre of the dry ingredients and add the buttermilk, tomatoes, eggs and oil. Mix quickly to just combine, spoon into the prepared tin and level the surface.

4 Bake in the oven for 20–25 minutes.

5 Turn out on to a wire rack and leave to cool slightly. When ready to serve, cut into eight pieces.

Yeast Free Bread

Fig and Rosemary Damper

Makes: *1 loaf* **Preparation time:** *25 minutes + 30–35 minutes baking*
Freezing: *recommended*

Damper is an Australian bread – a staple for campers.
Traditionally, pieces of dough are cooked over the dying embers
of the camp fire. This is a more luxurious version, flavoured with
sweet dried figs, walnuts and rosemary. It is great served anytime,
and hovers between a sweet and savoury bread.

350 g (12 oz) self-raising flour
80 g (3 oz) butter
½ teaspoon salt
80 g (3 oz) dried soft figs, chopped
40 g (1½ oz) walnuts, chopped, plus extra for
  the topping
2 teaspoons fresh rosemary, chopped, plus
  extra for the topping
1 tablespoon runny honey
175 ml (6 fl oz) semi-skimmed milk, plus extra
  to glaze

1 Preheat the oven to Gas Mark 7/220°C/425°F.
  Grease a baking sheet.

2 Place the flour in a bowl and rub in the butter.
  Mix in the salt, figs, walnuts and rosemary.
  Add the honey and milk and mix to a soft
  dough.

3 Turn out on to a floured work surface and
  work lightly to make a smooth ball of dough.

4 Transfer to the baking sheet and press down
  to make an 18 cm (7 inch) circle. Score the
  top into eight sections. Brush with some milk
  and sprinkle with walnuts and a little chopped
  rosemary.

5 Bake for 10 minutes, then reduce the
  temperature to Gas Mark 4/180°C/350°F.
  Bake for a further 20–25 minutes or until the
  loaf is golden and sounds hollow when tapped
  on the bottom.

6 Transfer to a wire rack to cool.

Yeast Free Bread

Potato Farls

Makes: *4 breads* **Preparation time:** *30 minutes + cooling + 6–8 minutes cooking*
Freezing: *not recommended*

Farls are a form of Irish soda bread, cooked on a griddle or skillet.
They are at their best made with freshly cooked potato and are
great for brunch, topped with an egg and crispy dry cured bacon.

300 g (10 oz) floury potatoes, peeled and
  chopped
1 tablespoon butter
1 medium egg, beaten
115 g (4 oz) plain all-purpose white flour
¼ teaspoon bicarbonate of soda
¼ teaspoon salt
2 teaspoons sunflower oil

1 Place the potatoes in a saucepan, cover with
  water and bring to the boil. Simmer for 15–20
  minutes until tender. Drain well.

2 Add the butter to the potatoes and mash until
  smooth. Allow to cool – just warm is fine.

3 Beat the egg into the potato mixture. Sift
  together the flour, bicarbonate of soda and
  salt and stir into the potato.

4 Flour a work surface well. Tip out the farl
  mixture and, with heavily floured hands, pat
  into a 20 cm (8 inch) circle, 5 mm (¼ inch)
  thick. Alternatively, roll out with a rolling pin.
  Using a sharp knife, cut into quarters.

5 Heat a 23 cm (9 inch) griddle pan or skillet
  over a fairly low heat.

6 Pour the oil on to the griddle pan and allow
  to heat for 30 seconds. Carefully transfer the
  farls to the griddle, arranging in a single layer.
  Cook for 3–4 minutes, until puffy and golden.
  Turn over and cook for a further 3–4 minutes
  on the other side. Serve at once.

Yeast Free Bread

Mushroom and Taleggio Scone Based Pizzas

Makes: *2 pizzas* **Preparation time:** *30 minutes + 12–15 minutes baking*
Freezing: *not recommended*

These pizzas are made with a scone base, rather than bread dough. Customise with your favourite toppings or add grated Parmesan or dried herbs to the scone base mixture.

2 tablespoons butter
3 large flat field mushrooms, approximately
 175 g (6 oz), sliced
1 garlic clove, sliced
400 g can chopped tomatoes
1 teaspoon tomato purée
¼ teaspoon dried mixed herbs
salt, freshly ground black pepper and a pinch
 of sugar
4 teaspoons extra virgin olive oil
25 g (1 oz) baby spinach leaves, washed and
 dried
115 g (4 oz) Taleggio or Comté cheese, thinly
 sliced
For the scone base:
350 g (12 oz) self-raising white flour
¼ teaspoon salt
good pinch of cayenne pepper
50 g (2 oz) butter
approximately 200 ml (7 fl oz) semi-skimmed
 milk

1 Preheat the oven to Gas Mark 8/230°C/450°F. Grease two baking sheets.

2 Melt the butter in a pan, add the mushrooms and garlic and fry for 3–4 minutes until the mushrooms have re-absorbed their liquid. Leave to cool.

3 Pour the tomatoes into a sieve and drain well. Stir the tomato purée, herbs, seasoning and a pinch of sugar into the tomato pulp.

4 Make the scone base. Place the flour, salt and cayenne pepper in a bowl and rub in the butter. Make a well in the centre and gradually blend in enough milk to make a soft dough.

5 Turn out on to a lightly floured work surface and work gently until smooth. Divide into two. Form each into a round and roll out into 25 cm (10 inch) circles. Place one on each baking sheet.

6 Brush the top of the scones with a little oil, reserving the rest for finishing off. Spread the tomato mixture to the edges. Scatter the spinach leaves over the top, then the cooked mushrooms followed by the cheese. Drizzle a little oil over each pizza.

7 Bake towards the top of the oven for 12–15 minutes until the crusts are golden and the cheese is bubbling. Serve at once.

Yeast Free Bread

Bacon and Cheddar Loaf

Makes: *1 loaf* **Preparation time:** *25 minutes + 35–45 minutes baking*
Freezing: *not recommended*

Gluten and wheat free flour often contains potato flour, which works exceptionally well with bacon and cheese. Spring onions, softened in the bacon fat, gives this bread plenty of flavour. Before baking, score the dough into sections so that, once baked, people can help themselves by breaking off a piece.

80–115 g (3–4 oz) dry cured smoked streaky bacon, finely snipped
1 bunch of spring onions, thinly sliced
225 g (8 oz) wheat and gluten free plain white flour
1 tablespoon wheat and gluten free baking powder
1 teaspoon dry English mustard powder
¼ teaspoon salt
good pinch of cayenne pepper
80 g (3 oz) mature Cheddar cheese, finely grated
175 ml (6 fl oz) semi-skimmed milk, plus a little extra for brushing

1 Fry the bacon in a non-stick pan until it crisps up and is tinged brown. Reduce the heat and add the spring onions. Cook for 1–2 minutes to soften, remove from the heat and leave to cool.

2 Preheat the oven to Gas Mark 5/190°C/375°F. Grease a baking sheet.

3 In a mixing bowl, sift together the flour, baking powder, mustard powder, salt and cayenne pepper. Stir in most of the cheese and the cooled bacon and onion mixture. Make a well in the centre and add the milk. Mix to a soft dough.

4 Turn out on to a lightly floured work surface and work gently to just bring the dough together in a ball.

5 Place on the baking sheet and flatten slightly. Score the top into 6–8 segments. Brush with milk and scatter with the remaining cheese.

6 Bake for 35–45 minutes until golden. Cool on a wire rack.

Yeast, Wheat and Gluten Free Bread

Apricot, Cardamom and Green Tea Teabread

Makes: *1 loaf* **Preparation time:** *25 minutes + overnight soaking + 1¼ hours baking*
Freezing: *recommended*

This teabread is made with yogurt, giving it a fairly dense, almost pudding-like texture. It is also very moist as the apricots are soaked overnight in hot tea. A fruit or flower tea of your choice gives the loaf an aromatic scent.

225 g (8 oz) semi-dried apricots, finely chopped
300 ml (½ pint) strong, hot green tea with jasmine
175 g (6 oz) plain flour
115 g (4 oz) fine wholemeal flour
2 teaspoons baking powder
115 g (4 oz) unsalted butter
115 g (4 oz) caster sugar
40 g (1½ oz) pistachios
1 tablespoon cardamom seeds, husks removed and ground
150 ml (¼ pint) natural yogurt
1 medium egg, beaten
For the topping:
1–2 tablespoons apricot jam, sieved and warmed
2 semi-dried apricots, finely chopped
a handful of pistachios, finely chopped

1 Place the apricots in a bowl, pour over the hot tea, cover and soak overnight to plump up.

2 Preheat the oven to Gas Mark 4/180°C/350°F. Grease and line a 900 g (2 lb) loaf tin.

3 Combine the flours and baking powder in a bowl and rub in the butter. Stir in the sugar, pistachios and ground cardamom. Make a well in the centre and add the soaked apricots, yogurt and egg. Mix the ingredients just enough to combine and spoon into the prepared tin.

4 Bake in the oven for about 1¼ hours, covering the top with foil after an hour. Test to see if the bread is done by inserting a skewer, which should come out clean.

5 Remove from the oven and leave in the tin for 15 minutes before turning out on to a wire rack to cool.

6 Brush with a little warmed apricot jam and sprinkle with the chopped apricots and pistachios. Brush again lightly with apricot jam.

Tip: This teabread is best kept in the fridge because of its yogurt content.

Yeast Free Bread

Basic Wheat and Gluten Free White Bread

Makes: *1 loaf* **Preparation time:** *30 minutes + proving + 25–30 minutes baking*
Freezing: *recommended*

It is useful to have a plain loaf for everyday eating. This recipe makes use of potato and rice flours, which are available from larger supermarkets and health food shops. Xanthan gum is a gluten replacer that can also be found in health food shops or on the Internet.

225 g (8 oz) rice flour (a blend of white and brown)
50 g (2 oz) potato flour
50 g (2 oz) ground almonds
1 tablespoon sugar
½ teaspoon salt
1½ teaspoons fast action dried yeast
1 tablespoon xanthan gum
½ teaspoon bicarbonate of soda
2 medium eggs, beaten
1 teaspoon cider vinegar
5 tablespoons sunflower oil
250 ml (9 fl oz) warm semi-skimmed milk

1 Grease a 900 g (2 lb) loaf tin.

2 Combine the flours in a mixing bowl with the ground almonds, sugar, salt, yeast, xanthan gum and bicarbonate of soda. Make a well in the centre and add the beaten eggs, vinegar, oil and milk. Mix until smooth. The mixture will be quite stiff, but continue beating as best you can for 3–4 minutes.

3 Spoon the mixture into the prepared tin and level the surface. Cover and leave to prove (page 8) in a warm place until doubled in size (about 1–1¼ hours).

4 Preheat the oven to Gas Mark 7/220°C/425°F.

5 Bake in the preheated oven for 25–30 minutes until golden.

6 Remove from the tin and leave to cool on a wire rack.

Tip: Beating by hand is quite hard work, so use a mixer if you have one!

Wheat and Gluten Free Bread

Fennel Seed Flatbreads

Makes: *3 flatbreads* **Preparation time:** *20 minutes + proving + 12–15 minutes baking*
Freezing: *not recommended*

Flatbreads are wonderful for mopping up the juices of a casserole or curry. They are best eaten warm, soon after baking, otherwise they become rather dry. If you are not particularly keen on fennel, try another seed, such as sesame or caraway, or a sprinkling of dried herbs instead.

300 g (10 oz) wheat and gluten free white bread flour
1 teaspoon sugar
½ teaspoon salt
1 teaspoon fast action dried yeast
2 tablespoons olive oil
1 medium egg, beaten
175 ml (6 fl oz) warm water
For the topping:
milk, for brushing
¾ teaspoon fennel seeds

1 Combine the flour, sugar, salt and yeast in a bowl. Make a well in the centre and add the oil, egg and water. Stir the mixture with a wooden spoon until it all comes together.

2 Oil a bowl and transfer the dough into it. Cover and leave in a warm place to prove (page 8) for 1 hour.

3 Grease two or three baking sheets.

4 With well-floured hands, divide the dough into three. On a floured surface, roll out each piece into a 18 cm (7 inch) circle approximately 5 mm (¼ inch) thick. Space well apart on the baking sheets. Cover and prove for 30 minutes until slightly puffy.

5 Preheat the oven to Gas Mark 7/220°C/425°F.

6 Brush the circles with a little milk and sprinkle with the fennel seeds, pressing them down lightly. Bake for 12–15 minutes until beginning to colour.

7 Transfer to a wire rack and serve warm.

Wheat and Gluten Free Bread

Peshwari Mini Naans

Makes: *12 naans* **Preparation time:** *20 minutes + proving + 12 minutes grilling*
Freezing: *recommended*

These little flat breads are filled with coconut and sultanas, giving them a surprising, delicious sweetness. Serve as an accompaniment to spicy stews or make up mini ones and use as a base for canapés.

450 g (1 lb) wheat and gluten free white bread
  flour
2 teaspoons sugar
½ teaspoon salt
1½ teaspoons fast action dried yeast
1 teaspoon wheat and gluten free baking
  powder
1 teaspoon black onion seeds
2 tablespoons chopped fresh coriander
4 tablespoons natural yogurt
1 medium egg, beaten
25 g (1 oz) butter, melted, plus extra for
  brushing
200–225 ml (7–8 fl oz) hand-hot water
For the filling:
40 g (1½ oz) desiccated coconut
3 tablespoons sultanas

1 Combine the flour, sugar, salt, yeast, baking
  powder, onion seeds and coriander in a bowl.
  Make a well in the centre and add the yogurt,
  egg, butter and water. Mix to a soft dough.

2 Turn out on to a lightly floured work surface
  and form into a smooth ball. (This flour does
  not require kneading.) Place in an oiled bowl,
  cover and leave to prove (page 8) in a warm
  place for about 1 hour.

3 Grease two baking sheets.

4 Lightly knead (page 8) the dough just to knock
  out the air. Divide into 12 equal pieces. Using
  well-floured hands, shape each into a 10 cm
  (4 inch) disc.

5 Mix together the coconut and sultanas. Place
  a little of the filling mixture in the middle of a
  circle of dough. Fold the dough over to form
  a semicircle and press the edges to seal. (You
  don't need any water.) Pat the dough out to
  form an oval shape about 10 cm (4 inches)
  long and 5 mm (¼ inch) thick. Place on the
  baking sheet and repeat with the remaining
  discs. Cover and leave to prove until puffy.

6 Preheat the grill to its highest setting and grill
  the breads for 3 minutes on each side.

7 Serve brushed with melted butter.

Tip: Wheat and gluten free products do
tend to dry out quickly, so eat on the day of
baking.

Wheat and Gluten Free Bread

Banana and Chocolate Drop Cake

Makes: *1 loaf* **Preparation time:** *20 minutes + proving + 40–45 minutes baking*
Freezing: *recommended*

This bread is more like a cake. It keeps very well so you may want to double the quantities and freeze half.

225 g (8 oz) wheat and gluten free white bread flour
50 g (2 oz) muscovado sugar
¼ teaspoon salt
¾ teaspoon fast action dried yeast
50 g (2 oz) milk chocolate drops
50 g (2 oz) unsalted butter, melted
1 ripe banana, mashed
125 ml (4 fl oz) warm semi-skimmed milk
1 medium egg, beaten
¼ teaspoon vanilla essence
For the glaze:
2 tablespoons granulated sugar
4 tablespoons water

1 Grease and base line a 450 g (1 lb) loaf tin.

2 Combine the flour, sugar, salt, yeast, and chocolate drops in a bowl. Make a well in the middle and add the melted butter, mashed banana, milk, egg and vanilla essence. Beat with a wooden spoon until smooth.

3 Spoon the mixture into the prepared tin and level the surface, making a slight indent in the centre. Cover and leave to prove (page 8) in a warm place until doubled in size.

4 Preheat the oven to Gas Mark 6/200°C/400°F.

5 Make the glaze by dissolving the sugar in the water in a pan. Bring to the boil and simmer for 1 minute. Allow to cool.

6 Bake the loaf for 40–45 minutes. Remove from the oven and run a knife around the edge of the loaf. Leave in the tin for 5 minutes before turning out on to a wire rack.

7 Brush with the sugar glaze while still warm. Leave to cool.

Wheat and Gluten Free Bread

White Spelt 'Daisy' Rolls

Makes: *10 rolls* **Preparation time:** *15 minutes + proving + 12–15 minutes baking*
Freezing: *recommended*

This recipe is in this chapter because spelt is a 'true' cereal, not a modified one. Some people who are unable to tolerate wheat may therefore be able to eat spelt. White spelt flour is available from good health food shops, but it is expensive, as quite an intensive milling process is necessary to extract all the bran and wheat germ from the grain. The result is a creamy, cakey flour.

450 g (1 lb) white spelt flour
25 g (1 oz) butter
115 g (4 oz) barley flakes
1 teaspoon sugar
1 teaspoon salt
1 teaspoon fast action dried yeast
300 ml (½ pint) hand-hot water

1 Place the flour in a bowl and rub in the butter. Stir in the barley flakes, sugar, salt and yeast. Make a well in the centre and add the water to make a soft dough.

2 Turn out on to an unfloured work surface and knead (page 8) for 4–5 minutes only. Cover and leave in a warm place to prove (page 8) until doubled in size.

3 Grease two baking sheets.

4 Divide the dough into 10 pieces. Form each into a ball, flatten slightly then make five cuts with scissors, almost through to the centre, so that you have a 'daisy' effect. Place well apart on the baking sheets, cover and prove until doubled in size.

5 Preheat the oven to Gas Mark 7/220°C/425°F.

6 Bake the rolls for 12–15 minutes until golden. Cool on a wire rack.

Tips: Spelt flour has a more delicate gluten structure than wheat, so only requires 4–5 minutes kneading and does not take so long to prove.

The barley flakes give this bread a lovely crunchy, slightly chewy texture. They do, however, contain some gluten, so if you are worried about this omit them.

Index